The new police in nineteenth-century England

Focusing on the evolution of a policed society in nineteenth-century England by examining the arguments surrounding police reforms, the development of police forces and police work, and the popular response to the 'rozzers' as they were widely known, David Taylor provides an up-to-date introduction which sets the development of modern policing in the wider social and economic context of an urbanising and industrialising society.

The study of popular responses highlights the ambivalence that surrounded the new police and the continuing, often vicious, opposition to the police in many parts of urban and rural England which frustrated the hopes of police reformers and their supporters. It also throws new light on the hitherto neglected experiences and rewards enjoyed by the police themselves.

NEW FRONTIERS IN HISTORY

series editors

Mark Greengrass
Department of History, Sheffield University

John Stevenson
Worcester College, Oxford

This important series reflects the substantial expansion that has occurred in the scope of history syllabuses. As new subject areas have emerged and syllabuses have come to focus more upon methods of historical enquiry and knowledge of source materials, a growing need has arisen for correspondingly broad-ranging textbooks.

New Frontiers in History provides up-to-date overviews of key topics in British, European and world history, together with accompanying source material and appendices. Authors focus upon subjects where revisionist work is being undertaken, providing a fresh viewpoint which will be welcomed by students and sixth-formers. The series also explores established topics which have attracted much conflicting analysis and require a synthesis of the state of the debate.

Published titles

C. J. Bartlett Defence and diplomacy: Britain and the Great Powers, 1815–1914

Jeremy Black The politics of Britain, 1688–1800

Paul Bookbinder Weimar Germany: the Republic of the reasonable

Michael Braddick The nerves of state: taxation and the financing of the English state, 1558–1714

Michael Broers Europe after Napoleon: Revolution, reaction and romanticism, 1814–1848

David Brooks The age of upheaval: Edwardian politics, 1899–1914

Carl Chinn Poverty amidst prosperity: the urban poor in England, 1834–1914

Conan Fischer The rise of the Nazis

T. A. Jenkins Parliament, party and politics in Victorian Britain

Keith Laybourn The General Strike of 1926

Panikos Panayi Immigrants, minorities and British society, 1815–1919

Daniel Szechi The Jacobites: Britain and Europe, 1688–1788

John Whittam Fascist Italy

Forthcoming titles

Joanna Bourke Production and reproduction: working women in Britain, 1860–1960

Ciaran Brady The unplanned conquest: social changes and political conflict in sixteenth-century Ireland

Susan-Mary Grant The American Civil War and Reconstruction

Evan Mawdsley The Soviet Union 1922–1956

Neville Kirk The rise of Labour, 1850–1920

Alan O'Day Irish Home Rule

The new police in nineteenth-century England
Crime, conflict and control

David Taylor

Manchester University Press

Manchester and New York

Distributed exclusively in the USA by St. Martin's Press

Copyright © David Taylor 1997

Published by Manchester University Press
Oxford Road, Manchester M13 9NR, UK
and Room 400, 175 Fifth Avenue, New York, NY 10010, USA

Distributed exclusively in the USA by St. Martin's Press, Inc.,
175 Fifth Avenue, New York, NY 10010, USA

British Library Cataloguing-in-Publication Data
A catalogue record for this book is available from the British Library

Library of Congress Cataloging-in-Publication Data
Taylor, David, 1946 May 10–
    The new police in nineteenth-century England : crime, conflict,
and control / David Taylor
        p.   cm. – (New frontiers in history)
    Includes bibliographical references and index.
    ISBN 0-7190-4728-5. – ISBN 0-7190-4729-3
    1. Police–England–History–19th century.   2. Law enforcement–
England–History–19th century.   3. England–History–19th century.
I. Title.   II. Series.
HV8195.T39 1997
36.2'0942'09034–dc20   96-32187
                                                          CIP

ISBN 0 7190 4728 5 *hardback*
      0 7190 4729 3 *paperback*

First published 1997

00 99 98 97   10 9 8 7 6 5 4 3 2 1

Printed by Bell & Bain Ltd, Glasgow

Dedicated to the memory of my parents, John and Jean Taylor

Contents

Contents

Tables

Acknowledgements

I owe a debt of gratitude to numerous people who made possible the writing of this book. The various librarians and archivists, particularly those at the Cleveland County Archive, Middlesbrough, the West Yorkshire County Archive, Wakefield, and the university libraries of Huddersfield and Teesside, who made my task much lighter through their knowledge and good nature, deserve particular praise. So too do those many scholars of whose work I have made use. The endnote references do scarce justice to the debt I owe.

I would like to thank the following for granting permission to use extracts from their works: the editor of *Historical Research* for the extract from D. Philips and R. D. Storch, 'Whigs and coppers: the Grey ministry's police scheme, 1832', *Historical Research*, 1994; Brewin Books for the extract from D. J. Elliot, *Policing Shropshire, 1836–1967*, 1984; Dorset Publishing for the extract from M. Hann, *Policing Victorian Dorset*; Landy Publishing for the extract from B. Dobson, *Policing in Lancashire, 1839–1989*, 1989; Prentice Hall for extracts from C. Emsley, *The English Police: A Political and Social History*, 1991; and Routledge and Kegan Paul for the extract from C. Steadman, *Policing the Victorian Community*, 1984. The author and the publisher apologise for any inadvertent infringement of copyright. In every case, documents have been fully attributed and every effort has been made to trace the copyright owner.

I am also very grateful to Professor Clive Emsley of the Open University and Dr Peter Gurney of Huddersfield University for making time available to read and comment on a draft of this book. The present text is better for their kind but critical comments. Even greater is the debt to my colleague Professor Keith Laybourn. His comments were, as ever, invaluable, but without his friendly encouragement I would never have pursued the idea which has now become this book.

Finally, my deepest thanks go to my wife, Thelma. As well as reading each draft with the shrewd eye of the educated layperson, she provided the support and encouragement, during very difficult times, without which this book would not have been completed.

1

Interpretations, problems and themes

the posters telling of cricket matches and Royal Weddings, the men in
bowler hats, the pigeons in Trafalgar Square, the red buses, the blue
policemen. (George Orwell, *Homage to Catalonia*, 1938, chapter 14)

George Orwell's response on his return from Spain captures the
centrality of the 'bobby' in the popular image of England. Yet it is
all too easy to lose sight of the fact that he, and before the First
World War there were only policemen, was a relatively recent
arrival on the national scene. In the early nineteenth century,
England was lightly policed, for the most part, by the traditional
system of the parish constable. There was widespread opposition
to the idea of a paid police force. Fears of continental-style
despotism threatening the liberties of the English people were to be
found among a wide cross-section of society, from working-class
radicals to provincial gentry. By the early twentieth century,
England was a policed society with paid, uniformed and bureaucratically controlled police forces for every county and borough.
Widespread hostility had been replaced by a widespread acceptance of the police which contrasted not only with earlier attitudes
but also with the actions that had greeted the arrival of the so-
called 'new police'.

The development of modern policing and the evolution of a
policed society are of fundamental importance to an understanding
of the society in which we live. Many of the issues which divided

nineteenth-century politicians and commentators remain contentious today. Historians, however, are divided in their interpretation of these events. Broadly speaking, three schools of thought can be identified.[1] The first, usually described as the orthodox or Whig interpretation, dates back to the earliest histories of the police, written at the beginning of the twentieth century, and is to be seen in the numerous writings of Charles Reith in the mid-twentieth century and, most notably, in the impressively researched writings of Sir Leon Radzinowicz and the influential survey history of the police by T. A. Critchley.[2] Significantly written at a time when the public's estimation of the police was at its zenith, this interpretation is essentially conservative and adopts a consensual model of society. It depicts a simple, straight-line development of policing from the first reformers (and indeed their heroic if unsuccessful predecessors) to the present day. The underlying assumption is that modernisation was unproblematic and that the police, as they developed, represented the most appropriate, most progressive and most effective response to the problems of society. The new police, from their first appearance in London, were a logical response to the problems of the day and the London model was quickly adopted in the rest of the country and accepted by the populace as a whole, or so the argument runs.

This Whiggish view of police history, underpinned by an unproblematic notion of modernisation, is unsatisfactory in a number of important ways. Put simply, it offers an oversimplified and distorted picture. It fails to take into account the diversity and legitimacy of opinions that existed among opponents and proponents of police reform. It does not give sufficient weight to the changing context in which police reform developed and to the impact of short-term and 'accidental' factors. Furthermore, this interpretation exaggerates the contrast between the 'old' and the 'new' police, underestimates the time needed to develop efficient police forces after their initial formation, and gives a misleading impression of the speed with which the new police were accepted. Indeed, the persistence of varied and often violent responses to the new police has been central to the second, or revisionist, school of thought.

Rejecting the conservative assumptions of the orthodox school and often looking for inspiration to Engels and Marx, the revisionist school offers a starkly different interpretation. Theirs is based on a conflict model of society, which emphasises the moral as well as the physical threat of the working classes. The advent and impact of the new police are presented in terms of the bourgeoisie seeking to extend its control over the dangerous classes.[3] Notions of social control are seen to dominate the thinking of police reformers, chief constables and their supporters. At the same time, the police are seen to have a missionary role as the front-line figures, enforcing 'respectable' codes of behaviour on 'rough' society.

The revisionist interpretation offers a more sophisticated analysis of the development of policing by relating the emergence and impact of the new police in a more explicit manner to changing economic and political circumstances. The awareness of conflicting opinions and values, themselves rooted in the profound and rapid changes of the early nineteenth century, is a significant advance on the orthodox interpretation with its simplistic view of the triumph of good over evil. However, it is not without its problems. It too offers an oversimplified and distorted view. The distinction between 'rough' and 'respectable' is by no means clear cut. More importantly, the concept of social control has come in for considerable criticism. As F. M. L. Thompson has pointed out, used indiscriminately and uncritically, to explain everything, the concept explains nothing about social relations.[4] More specifically, the notion of social control implies a degree of agreement among the propertied classes that simply did not exist. While there was a fluctuating but continuing concern over the 'problem' of the working classes, there were lively debates over both the need for and the most appropriate form of action to be taken. Indeed, attitudes towards sensitive issues such as popular recreation often cut across, rather than ran along, class lines.[5] Furthermore, the social control argument is also open to the criticism of confusing intention with outcome, though this does not apply with such force to revisionist historians who have emphasised the extent of popular opposition and resistance to the 'domestic missionary' role of the new police. Finally, by seeing the police as class warriors, fighting to enforce bourgeois values, there is a real danger of overlooking important variations in police attitudes. Undoubtedly some chief constables were unequivocal in their desire to clean up their 'patch' but others took a more pragmatic approach, turning a blind eye to immoral behaviour, such as drunkenness or prostitution, if it did not involve violence or blatantly indecorous behaviour on the streets. As for the ordinary police constable, the evidence of his behaviour on many occasions shows clearly that he not only sympathised with but also participated in some of the activities he was supposed to suppress!

The growing body of detailed research has cast considerable doubt on the comfortable verities of orthodox and revisionist historians. These more recent writings have adopted a more complex stance, recognising the variations that were to be found in different parts of the country and also between and within classes.[6] The proliferation of local studies has greatly increased our knowledge of the evolution of the new police but it has also militated against a more general interpretation. However, there have been two recent attempts to synthesise recent research. Robert Reiner, concerned more with policing in the late twentieth century, provides an incisive critique of the historical literature, from which he derives a 'neo-Reithian synthesis', which acknowledges the successes eventually achieved by police reformers but which also 'recognises that policing is embedded in a social order riven by structured bases of conflict, not fundamental integration' and in which policing may be 'more or less harmonious, or overtly oppressive'.[7] Clive Emsley, in a wide-ranging survey based on an extensive range of archival sources, similarly seeks to offer an interpretation 'critical of the traditional Whig view, but equally sceptical of the notion that the police can best be understood as an instrument of class power'. Rather, while recognising their power of coercion, the police, and the law generally, are seen as 'multi-faceted institutions used by Englishmen of all classes to oppose each other, to co-operate with, and to gain concessions from, each other'.[8] The present volume is written in the same spirit of sceptical synthesis. However, as will become apparent, there is not an easy and obvious balance to be struck.

Three main themes will be explored in this book. The first is concerned with the changing attitudes towards policing and the motives of the various reformers who were responsible for the key legislative changes that were implemented between 1829 and 1856. The second focuses upon the creation of county and borough police forces and the transformation from the ill-discipline and high turnover of the mid-nineteenth-century forces to the greater discipline and stability of the forces of the early twentieth century.

The third deals with the question of popular response and explores the change from the widespread hostility in the early years of the 1840s and 1850s to the greater degree of acceptance that was to be found in Edwardian England. Each of these themes has given rise to debate.

The advent of the 'new police' marked an important development in law enforcement in modern Britain. On that historians agree. However, the motives behind this departure remain a matter of dispute. For orthodox historians, the new police were the 'logical' response to the collapse of law and order and the rising tide of crime that threatened to overwhelm society in the early nineteenth century as industrialisation and urbanisation proceeded apace. Rising crime and the patent inadequacies of existing law-enforcement agents – the much ridiculed Charlies, or watchmen – necessitated a new form of control. Peel's new police, it is argued, were a rational and far-sighted response to a social problem that threatened all decent and law-abiding members of society.

There are major problems with such an argument. It is by no means clear that early-nineteenth-century England was facing a massive crime wave and, equally importantly, it is also unclear to what extent reformers were motivated by fear of crime. Further, despite the emphasis placed on the threat of crime, the orthodox view largely overlooks the public order problem of the time. In addition, the contrast between old and new forms of maintaining order is overdrawn. Even in parts of London, let alone in the rest of the country, the old police were far from being chronically inadequate, while the new police were less efficient in practice than the earlier police historians have maintained.

To revisionists, industrialisation and urbanisation were important but in another way. As a new class-based society emerged, the needs of bourgeois society, threatened by the turbulent masses increasingly concentrated in the burgeoning towns and cities, required a more effective form of social control. Peel's new police were, again, a rational and far-sighted response but this time to a problem that threatened one particular section of society. The problematic nature of the concept of social control has been discussed earlier but it is important to stress how this has led to an oversimplified view of the reformers' arguments. This has resulted, for example, in a neglect of those arguments that saw the development of policing more in administrative terms – a tidying

5

up of law enforcement in the name of efficiency – and, without denying a concern with crime control, locates the reform of policing in a wider process of state development.

It will be argued in chapter 2 that there was a continuing and complex debate about police reform, characterised by a wide range of concerns, ranging from fear of a growth in crime (especially theft in its various forms), to concerns about public order, public morality and the efficiency with which local government was conducted. Further, there was considerable debate as to the precise form that the new police should take. Diversity was the keynote of both theory and practice in the second quarter of the nineteenth century. There was nothing inevitable about the form of policing that was to develop after 1856.

The second major theme, the development of modern police forces, has been less the subject of debate, despite the intrinsic importance of the subject. Orthodox historians, emphasising the contrast between old and new police, have assumed that efficiency was achieved rapidly and gloss over some very real practical problems. Similarly, revisionist historians have not explored the question in any great detail despite rightly pointing to the problems that beset the early police forces. However, with one or two notable exceptions, little has been said about the problems facing the Victorian chief constable seeking to create an effective force, nor those facing the Victorian constable as he sought to make sense of his job.

A key element in the development of modern policing is the question of accountability. Orthodox historians have argued that the new police, based as they were on the older concept of the constable, were ultimately accountable to the people. In contrast, revisionists have strongly denied any idea of democratic account-ability. In the counties, some have argued, chief constables were drawn from the same class as and shared the views of the magistrates who appointed them, while in the boroughs the chief constables, as employees of the watch committees, were at the mercy of the middle classes, who dominated the local electorates and locally elected posts. Others have been more sceptical of the impact of watch committees and, instead, have argued that democratic control was undermined by the autonomy always enjoyed by county chief constables and acquired by borough chief constables by the late nineteenth century.

In chapter 3 it will be argued that the development of modern policing was shaped by a combination of economic and socio-cultural factors that led to the creation of a body of men and an ideology which in turn profoundly influenced the impact of the police and the response of the policed. Specifically, it will be shown that the creation of a network of efficient police forces was a long and complex process. The transition from instability to stability was the product of a variety of factors which affected the individual policeman. Improvements in real wages, changes in perception of the job and a growing sense of camaraderie born of being a group apart all played their part. At the same time, the distinctiveness that the ordinary constable felt in carrying out his day-to-day duties was replicated in the upper ranks of the force where the operational skills and judgements of the chief constable in particular gave an element of independence and autonomy.

The final theme, which explores the actions of the police and the reactions of the public to them, has given rise to the most heated debate. Once again, opinions have been shaped, to a large extent, by broader beliefs concerning the fundamental nature of nineteenth-century society: those believing in an underlying consensus took (and take) a fundamentally different view from those who saw (and see) conflict as the dominant social reality. For the former, the police were agents of order, working for the benefit of the law-abiding irrespective of class; for the latter, the police were agents of social control, enforcing the codes of behaviour of a hegemonic class. Finally, in the most recent writings of Reiner and Emsley the emphasis has been placed on the diversity of responses and the multi-usage nature of the police and the criminal justice system.

In discussing this question, it is useful to distinguish between a number of distinct but inter-related issues that divide both contemporary and historical opinion. First, there is the question of the functions of the new police: what precisely did the new police do? For the founding fathers of the Metropolitan Police Force and for later Whig historians, the police were first and foremost a crime-prevention force. Their responsibility was to protect all innocent members of society, no matter how humble, from the criminal. By enforcing the law the police, or so it was argued, brought a disproportionate benefit to the working classes, who lacked the strength to protect themselves from the depredations of the lawless. Furthermore, this public servant model was enhanced by a variety of other activities undertaken by the police. As inspectors of weights and measures, doubling up as firemen or acting as unofficial 'knockers-up' they provided the public with a service which led *The Times* in 1908 to refer to the London bobby as 'the true handyman of our streets, the best friend of a mass of people who have no other counsellor or protector'.[9]

However, the notion of the policeman as crime fighter is something of a myth. Clearly, the police did combat crime but it was by no means their only responsibility. Nonetheless, it did provide a powerful legitimising argument which glossed over other aspects of police work.[10] The orthodox interpretation, by emphasising the public servant role of the police, overlooks the more contentious aspects of police work, much of which was concerned with maintaining order and decorum on the streets of Victorian England. This led to a conflict of values as time-honoured popular practices were condemned and criminalised and hence, on many occasions, to physical conflict with the police, who were cast in the role of 'domestic missionaries', bringing the message of 'respectability' to 'rough' communities.

Considerations such as this have led revisionists to reject the comforting orthodox interpretations. Along with certain contemporary observers, they have argued that the police were more the agents of a ruling elite. Police work was as much about keeping the 'dangerous classes' under surveillance and control as about fighting crime. Organised labour as much as organised crime was the threat to be contained. In a similar vein, the enforcement of the law more often than not meant the enforcement of bye-laws intended to maintain decorum in the streets for the benefit of the middle classes. As Storch has argued, the new police were 'domestic missionaries' sent out to civilise darkest England as surely as the missionaries sent out to civilise darkest Africa.

Linked to this debate on the nature of policing is the question of the effectiveness and efficiency with which the police carried out their various duties. Whatever the intention of parliamentary reformers, of members of local watch committees, or even of chief constables, much depended upon the ability and determination with which ordinary policemen set about their various tasks. Contemporaries were divided in their assessments. For some, the new police represented good value for money, bringing a perceptible improvement in terms of crime control and street order.

8

Others were less impressed, feeling that the money spent was wasted on an inefficient body of men. Historians, insofar as they have considered the matter, have been similarly divided, with some seeing the police as effective enforcers of the law to some or all sectors of society and others seeing the police as ill-disciplined and largely inefficient, particularly in the early years.

Finally, there is the contentious issue of the response, or more accurately responses, of various sectors of the public. There is no doubting that the initial introduction of the new police was accompanied by controversy and conflict in many parts of the country. Historians differ in their interpretation of the nature and extent of the opposition to the new forces of law and order. The orthodox interpretation concedes initial unpopularity, especially in London, but sees this as the short-lived product of misguided beliefs about the purpose of the new police among the working classes and of better-founded fears among the criminal elements of the capital. After early hostilities, such as the disturbances at Cold Bath Fields in 1833, which led to the death of PC Culley, the value of the police to law-abiding Londoners was quickly appreciated by the middle classes and somewhat later by the working classes. By the end of the century the 'bobby' had been taken to the hearts of Londoners, at times seen as a figure of fun with a weakness for food and kitchen maids but also viewed with affection as a friend and protector. This pattern, or so it is argued by those who take an essentially consensual and Whiggish view of society and its development, was more or less repeated as new police forces were introduced in other parts of the country.

The orthodox interpretation has been rightly criticised for ignoring the extent of popular hostility in the mid-nineteenth century and for overlooking the persistence of hostility to the police in the late nineteenth and early twentieth centuries. However, the revisionist view is open to a number of important criticisms. There is a tendency to talk of working-class responses simply in terms of opposition. As will be argued in chapter 4, the reality was more complex. Undoubtedly, violence against the police was an enduring feature of Victorian society. In exceptional circumstances whole communities rose up against the new police, but one must not generalise from such spectacular and atypical events. Diversity, once again, is of the essence. Different sections of the working classes had differing views of the police, and even at an individual level there could be sharply different responses to the police depending upon the specific circumstances. Further, there is a danger of failing to distinguish with sufficient care between opposition to the police per se and opposition to unpopular policemen or to unpopular aspects of police work. While the distinction is not entirely clear cut, it will be argued that there was a shift from the former to the latter in the period under review.

In conclusion, it must be emphasised that the creation of a policed society with a network of county and borough police forces was one of the fundamental developments of Victorian England. However, this development was both complex and controversial. The Victorian debate on policing was lively and long lived. Moreover, many of the issues that proved to be contentious then were never fully resolved and remain with us as problematic issues today. With this heritage of ongoing and often heated dispute in mind, it is time to turn to the first major theme, that is, the debate over police reform.

Notes

1   As is so often the case, the identification of 'schools of thought' involves an element of oversimplification and hence caricature. The following criticisms should not obscure the fact that both orthodox and revisionist interpretations are often based on detailed archival work and show an appreciation of the complexities of historical change. However, one can identify underlying models of society and historical development which need to be subjected to close scrutiny. In addition, there is an element of arbitrariness in lumping together historians in different categories.

2   Captain W. L. Melville Lee, *A History of Police in England*, London, Methuen, 1901; C. Reith, *The Police Idea*, Oxford, Oxford University Press, 1938, *The British Police and the Democratic Ideal*, Oxford, Oxford University Press, 1943, *A Short History of the Police*, Oxford, Oxford University Press, 1948, and *A New Study of Police History*, London, Oliver & Boyd, 1956; L. Radzinowicz, *A History of English Criminal Law*, London, Stevens, vol. 1 1948, vol. 2 1956, vol. 3 1956, vol. 4 1968; T. A. Critchley, *A History of Police in England and Wales*, London, Constable, 1967.

3   Especially R. D. Storch, 'The plague of blue locusts: police reform and popular resistance in Northern England 1840–57', *International Review of Social History*, 20, 1975, and 'The policeman as domestic missionary', *Journal of Social History*, ix:4, 1976. See also A. Silver, 'The demand for order

in civil society', in D. Bordau, ed., *The Police*, New York, Wiley, 1967, and J. Foster, *Class Struggle in the Industrial Revolution*, London, Methuen, 1974.

4   F. M. L. Thompson, 'Social control in Victorian Britain', *Economic History Review*, 2nd series, 33, 1981.

5   See for example the substantial literature on working-class leisure, notably: A. P. Donajgrodzki, ed., *Social Control in Nineteenth-Century Britain*, London, Croom Helm, 1977; R. D. Storch, ed., *Popular Culture in Nineteenth-Century Britain*, London, Croom Helm, 1982; H. Cunningham, *Leisure in the Industrial Revolution*, London, Croom Helm, 1980.

6   See especially C. Steedman, *Policing and the Victorian Community: The Formation of English Provincial Police Forces, 1856–80*, London, Routledge, 1984; R. Swift, *Police Reform in Early Victorian York, 1838–1856*, York, University of York, Borthwick Papers, no. 73, 1988; R. Swift, 'Urban policing in early Victorian England, 1835–1856: a re-appraisal', *History*, 73, 1988; D. Taylor, 'Crime and policing in early Victorian Middlesbrough, 1835–55', *Journal of Regional and Local Studies*, 11, 1991.

7   R. Reiner, *The Politics of the Police*, 2nd edn, Hemel Hempstead, Harvester Wheatsheaf, 1992, p. 5.

8   C. Emsley, *The English Police: A Political and Social History*, Hemel Hempstead, Harvester Wheatsheaf, 1991, pp. 5–6.

9   *The Times*, 24 December 1908, p. 6.

10   V. A. C. Gatrell, 'Crime, authority and the policeman-state', in F. M. L. Thompson, ed., *Cambridge Social History*, vol. 3, Cambridge, Cambridge University Press, 1990.

2

The evolution of modern policing: legislative changes, 1829–56

A new force of police had to be found; it had to be invented. (Charles Reith, *A Short History of the British Police*, 1948, p. 4)

Introduction

Between 1829 and 1856 Parliament passed a series of acts which effectively brought into being the 'new police'. The process was a complex one, surrounded by controversy at the time, and subject to much debate later. In assessing the relative merits of these different arguments, through a detailed consideration of the evolution of the major pieces of legislation, the emphasis will be on the diversity of opinion and the absence of any consensus on the most appropriate form of policing. However, it is important, at the outset, to make some general observations on the manner in which the new police came into being and, in so doing, to highlight some of the major problems in explaining 'the birth of the blues'.

First, it is tempting, but misleading, to see police reform as a simple process of diffusion of a metropolitan model that dates from the 1829 Metropolitan Police Act, through the 1835 Municipal Corporations Act and the 1839 Rural Constabulary Act, and culminating in the 1856 County and Borough Police Act.[1] The reality is more complex, with alternative models and practices of policing co-existing and competing with each other during the first half of the nineteenth century. There was nothing inevitable about the development of policing in the early to mid-nineteenth century. A growing concern among local and national elites with the problem of crime is clear, as is the perceived need for an effective response, but both the form and timing of change are problematic and explanations will, necessarily, be complex.

Second, this 'problem–response' approach to the history of policing, while undoubtedly attractive and potentially fruitful, has its difficulties. The development of policing clearly cannot be considered in isolation from its wider context of socio-economic, political and administrative change, but it is essential to specify the precise links between the general problem and the particular solution that emerged. Careful local studies provide a useful antidote to overgeneralised and simplistic explanations but this approach can become *too* particular and lose sight not only of the wider context in which policy developed, as John Styles rightly notes, but also of the common concerns that were to be found in often markedly different circumstances.[2]

Again at the risk of oversimplification, it can be argued that the debate about policing was in essence concerned with the balance between liberty and order. Protagonists in the debate, be they interested primarily in London, one of the burgeoning and increasingly industrial towns, or a predominantly rural county, drew on a wide variety of arguments and evidence in seeking to strike the appropriate balance. In debating the problems of crime and order and in evaluating possible responses, decisions were made which were not simply the product of an evaluation of the 'threat' of crime in the locality at the time. The decision makers also drew on a view of English history and a belief in certain constitutional rights. In addition they had an awareness of current administrative and political possibilities, including a concern with financial implications.

Third, any explanation of change must be dynamic, to allow for the changing perceptions of crime, the threat that it posed to society and the need for changes in law enforcement. In contrast to debate in much of the eighteenth century, early-nineteenth-century discussions of crime were overlaid with wider concerns for order and stability in a visibly changing world. The tolerance of crime and disorder diminished as fears grew. Furthermore, new standards of behaviour led to new expectations that heightened the intolerance of crime and disorder.

Finally, in seeking to explain the emergence of the new police, it is important not to read back crudely from outcome to intention. It would be naive indeed to assume that the actual development of the new force was identical to the aspirations of the reformers. To put it somewhat flippantly, no one would seriously suggest that because policemen spent time helping old ladies across roads and restoring lost children to their parents this was the reason for their introduction.

London and the Metropolitan Police, 1829

Robert Peel, introducing his Metropolis Police Improvement Bill to the House of Commons in April 1829, argued that his proposed reforms were necessary to meet the growing threat to property and person in the capital which was clearly to be seen in the annual statistics of committals for trial. While recognising that some districts of London were adequately protected, he stressed the inability of existing law-enforcement officers to maintain acceptable levels of protection for the capital as a whole. As he was the main architect of reform, his words have to be considered carefully. For orthodox historians Peel's explanation provides clear evidence to support their general thesis of a rising tide of crime overwhelming incompetent, if not corrupt, watchmen. However, on closer examination there are difficulties in accepting this explanation as a complete answer, partly because both the elements on which it rests are flawed and partly because it fails to acknowledge other considerations.

Fears about rising levels of crime in London were not new. There was much concern in the 1780s and 1790s with 'the rapid and alarming increase in crimes and depredations in this city', as the mayor and aldermen of the City of London put it in their petition to the King in 1786.[3] Such fears were largely impressionistic but with the publication of annual crime statistics there was, or so it seemed, hard fact that brooked no argument. In reality, as some contemporary critics noted, the figures did not give a precise indication of change in the level of crime. Contrary to popular belief, crime statistics probably reveal more about the willingness and ability to prosecute than about the real incidence of crime. It is more than likely that the early nineteenth century witnessed an explosion in prosecutions rather than an explosion of crime.[4] There is clear evidence to suggest that courts were no longer viewed as a last resort, as had previously been the case, but were now being used by a wide section of the population, particularly in London.[5] Furthermore, the cost of prosecution had been reduced by a series of acts dating from the mid-eighteenth century which by 1788 ensured that prosecutors received expenses in all felony cases. This process continued and culminated in Peel's 1826 Criminal Justice Act, which provided for the payment of expenses for prosecutors and witnesses in all felonies and certain misdemeanours. While it is not possible to quantify the impact of these changes it is difficult to see them having anything other than an inflationary effect on the crime statistics.

However, to say that the official crime statistics were misleading does not end the question. Two further possibilities need to be considered. First, if contemporaries believed that the figures measured a genuine increase in crime, then that in itself becomes a crucial historical 'fact', irrespective of later judgements; and there is certainly evidence that points in that direction.[6] Second, even if contemporaries were sceptical of the figures, as indeed some were, they may have been unwilling to tolerate levels of crime and disorder that would have been acceptable in the previous century. We will never know how many people fell into each of these categories and, in many respects, this does not matter because the crucial point at issue is not the actual level but the *acceptable* level of crime. For whatever reason, a growing body of influential people felt that the levels of crime in London had reached unacceptable proportions and new action was now needed.

The second element in the orthodox argument is the incompetence of the parochial watchmen. Mercilessly lampooned in contemporary print, these men have entered the history books as physical and moral incompetents, at best figures of fun, more often worse.[7] However, recent research, most notably by Ruth Paley, reveals a different situation.[8] Rather than the static, incompetent and corrupt system depicted by orthodox historians, policing in pre-1829 London was more dynamic, more efficient and less venal than suggested by the supporters of Peel's Police Bill. In recruitment attention was paid to good character and physique. In addition, there was, invariably, an upper age limit. Although the watch was parish based, the problem of fragmentation was offset, in part at least, by the growing practice of inter-parochial co-operation. Moreover, oft-quoted contemporary critics, such as Colquhoun, are now seen to have been more marginal figures who enjoyed little support and exercised even less influence at the time. Furthermore, much of the evidence mustered in the late 1820s, and quoted uncritically later, was of a highly partisan nature, chosen for the express purpose of facilitating the passage of Peel's reform proposals. In the light of this evidence it is difficult to see the new police simply as a response to the failures of the old system.

Other explanations need to be found for the coming of the 1829 Metropolitan Police Act. Part of the answer lies with the concerns of Peel himself, but a more important part lies in the shift in attitudes that had taken place between the 1780s and the 1820s. Four critical elements are here entwined: a growing pre-occupation with crime as a manifestation of the problems associated with socio-economic change; changing standards of behaviour, which included a growing intolerance of violence, disorder and crime and a corresponding belief in the need for greater 'discipline' in society; a new perception of protection and punishment; and new expectations of the magistracy. Each point deserves detailed consideration.

Despite the riotous tradition of late-eighteenth-century London there was, as V. A. C. Gatrell has pointed out, a 'relative in-difference to crime as a "problem" ... and the terms in which crime might be debated as a "problem" were not yet formed'.[9] However, attitudes were to change from the 1780s onwards. While historians looking back on the late eighteenth century now comment on the evolutionary nature of social and economic change, contemporaries were struck by the scale and speed with which a familiar world was being eroded. Change could be viewed in a positive light: industrialisation and urbanisation were proof of society's inventiveness and civilisation. On the other hand, industrial and urban areas were sites of disorder – moral and physical swamps, as the contemporary phrase ran. Change had become the general condition: stability appeared threatened on all sides. As the towns and cities grew so the old vertical ties of deference were weakened, or so it was believed, and the stability of the social hierarchy was threatened. Crime took on a significance that went beyond its immediate impact. It was invested with new importance as the problems of modernisation became more apparent and as uncertainty increased. The criminal (not for the last time) became a convenient figure on whom to heap the worries and anxieties of modern society.

Moreover, the mounting crime figures of the early nineteenth century confirmed this sense of moral decay. Not surprisingly, as fears about social disorder increased so too did the value attached to the concept of order as opposed to liberty. Indeed, it was increasingly argued that liberty was dependent on order. The state was no longer automatically seen as an autocratic threat. For the elites of the late eighteenth century, the state was increasingly seen as an ally to help combat the threat of the urban masses. Beliefs in the benefits of discipline for the masses increased and fears about the loss of liberty diminished; but new agents would be required if the masses were to be disciplined.

At the same time, the tolerance of the elite for the riotous (as well as the criminal) poor was diminishing. This can be seen very graphically in the responses to the Gordon Riots of 1780 and in the early nineteenth century to disturbances following the Napoleonic Wars. In a yet more general sense, codes of behaviour were changing in a way that impinged on the collective activities of the labouring classes. Rioting in the defence of rights – a well established and accepted part of eighteenth-century social and political life, as E. P. Thompson and others have demonstrated[10] – was now seen as being subversive. Traditional recreations were likewise seen by some (though not all) members of the elite to be no longer acceptable. New ideas of property rights, new codes of behaviour that did not tolerate profanity, immorality and cruelty to animals, and a fear of the threat to law and order posed by the people *en masse* led to growing demands for the 'civilising' of the crowd. Once again, agents were needed to impose discipline and order.

The demand for new action also stemmed from a recon-sideration of the nature of punishment from the late eighteenth century onwards. At its most elevated, but probably most overstated, level there was a move away from the idea of deterrence based on the notion of exemplary but awful punish-ment, inflicted on a small number of convicted offenders, to a belief that proportionate punishment, which included the possi-bility of rehabilitation through the use of the penitentiary, was both rational and humane.[11] Similarly, under the influence of the ideas of

Beccaria and his followers, it was increasingly felt that the certainty of detection was the greater deterrent. More pragmatically, there was also a concern, particularly among shopkeepers and trades-people, that the law with its draconian penalties failed to give them the protection they required. Whether owing to the unwillingness of victims to prosecute or of juries to find guilty, too many thieves were going unpunished. That said, there was also a recognition that it was not simply impossible but also unacceptable to execute all offenders found guilty of capital offences.[12] Thus, a new system was required which would increase the likelihood of successful prosecution but reduce the severity of the punishment. Peel himself was well aware of such arguments and told the Commons that the continuation of law reform was dependent upon changes in policing.

Finally, we need to consider changing attitudes towards local administration in general and the magistracy in particular. Fears about the political dangers that might follow from bureaucratic expansion never disappeared but there are signs in and after the late eighteenth century of a new attitude towards administration and administrators. Impersonal public service and efficiency were the hallmarks of the new public service model of administration. Such standards were applied to the magistracy, albeit for reasons that remain unclear but which appear to have only partial reference to the problems of crime and public order. In this climate the idea of some form of 'bureaucratic police system, incorporating a stipendiary magistracy and a paid police force ... was likely to be prominent among the alternatives'.[13]

The impact of these factors on informed opinion can be seen from the following events. In June 1780 much of central London was in the hands of rioting crowds, who inflicted considerable damage on property, including symbolic attacks on prisons, the Bank of England and the houses of prominent figures, including magistrates and judges. Shelburne's denunciation of the 'imperfect, inadequate and wretched system' of policing in Westminster and Burke's condemnation of the Middlesex justices as 'the scum of the earth' played their part in bringing change.[14] However, despite demands for reform at the time of the Gordon Riots, it was not until 1785 that a bill was introduced by Pitt which would have created a single 'District of the Metropolis', including the City of London, with a police force under the control of three commissioners who, as justices of the peace, would have authority over the district and who would employ constables to prevent crime and to arrest offenders. Despite the scale of the Gordon Riots and the palpable failure of the magistrates, the bill was dropped within a week in the face of fierce opposition. In part this was based on narrow and selfish political grounds: the City of London bitterly opposed any infringement of its rights. However, opposition was more widespread. Politicians and the press railed against the threat of tyrannical French practices being imported into England. As the *Daily Universal Register* argued:

> Although many inconveniences arise from an excess of liberty in this country, yet they are so greatly overbalanced by the advantages, that we cannot be too careful to preserve a blessing which distinguishes us from all the world.... Our constitution can admit nothing like a French police ... [the] bill intended to amend the *police*, if passed into a law it would destroy the *liberty of the subject*.[15]

Such sentiments could be found later in the century, most eloquently in Charles James Fox's opposition to the 1792 Middlesex Justices Act, which created seven police offices for London, with three stipendiary magistrates and six paid police officers at each. However, by the middle of the next century such arguments no longer carried the same widespread support. Nonetheless, it would be foolish to underestimate such attitudes. As late as 1812, and despite the near panic created by the multiple killings in Wapping known as the Ratcliffe Highway murders, the Earl of Dudley could argue that he 'would rather half a dozen people's throats should be cut in Ratcliffe Highway every three or four years than to be subject to domiciliary visits, spies, and all the rest of Fouche's contrivances'.[16] Whether such a sentiment would have been welcomed in Wapping remains a moot point!

And even as late as 1822 the Select Committee established by Peel to look into policing arrangements in London could come to the conclusion that:

> It is difficult to reconcile an effective system of police with that perfect freedom of action and exemption from interference, which are the great privileges and blessing of society in this country; and your Committee think that the forfeiture or curtailment of such advantages would be too great a sacrifice for improvements in police, or facilities

in detection of crime, however desirable in themselves if abstractedly considered.[17]

However, policing practice had changed. The 1792 act, initially intended for only three years, was renewed annually until 1839. Moreover, the number of police officers in the metropolis had been increased. By the early nineteenth century each police office had twelve, instead of the original six, police officers. The Bow Street Office, itself dating from 1750, had introduced a horse and foot patrol in 1805 and further changes took place in the 1820s. On the eve of Peel's reform, in 1828, the horse patrol comprised fifty-four men and six officers; the dismounted patrol eighty-nine men and twelve officers; the night foot patrol eighty-two men and eighteen officers; and the day patrol twenty-four men and three officers.[18] Attitudes had also changed. For reasons discussed above, there was a growing concern with the threat posed by crime and a recognition that action was now needed, in London at least. More importantly, a growing number of people, not least Peel, were worried by the problem of public order and the inadequacy of the army and yeomanry as means of containment. In June 1820 the Duke of Wellington, concerned with signs of mutiny in the Guards at a time when the loyalty of the troops was of paramount importance, wrote to Lord Liverpool that, 'in my opinion the Government ought, without the loss of a moment's time, to adopt measures to form either a police in London or military corps, which should be of a different description from the regular military force, or both'.[19]

Peel, however, was the key individual. Having served as Chief Secretary in Ireland, he came to the Home Office with considerable experience of policing and police reform, albeit in very different circumstances to those he faced in England. He came to office following the resignation of Sidmouth in the aftermath of the disturbances that surrounded Queen Caroline's return to England in June 1820. Popular support, considerable when she first landed, increased during the parliamentary divorce proceedings and reached a peak following her death in August 1821. Special precautions were taken to ensure the untroubled passage of her funeral cortege through London. Within the metropolis five military regiments were put on alert while over 9,000 more troops were moved into the Home Counties.[20] Attempts to keep the cortege out of the City of London were thwarted by the people, despite troops firing on the crowd to maintain control. It was clear to all that 'the Mob' had triumphed over the military. For Peel, newly in office, an alternative had to be found.

Despite the rebuff by the 1822 Select Committee, Peel vowed to establish 'a vigorous, preventive police, consistent with the free principles of our free constitution'[21] and set about developing a government-directed police force for London that drew upon his experience of policing in Ireland. Although he was to make great play of the increase in crime in the capital, it seems clear that Peel was primarily concerned with the threat posed by political radicalism. His first fully fledged plan was drawn up in late 1826. The proposals were very similar to the Dublin police measures of 1786 and 1808. The fall of the Liverpool government meant that nothing came of these proposals but, on his return to the Home Office in January 1828, Peel took up again the question of metropolitan policing. The Select Committee of that year, effectively a mouthpiece for Peel's views, recommended the establishment of a single metropolitan police district and a police officer directly under the control of the Home Secretary. As Palmer notes, the proposals are identical to the Dublin police established in 1808, except that the latter refer to Lord Lieutenant rather than Home Secretary.[22]

The Metropolis Police Improvement Bill was introduced into the Commons on 15 April 1829 and, somewhat surprisingly, given past passions, passed through Parliament with virtually no discussion. Undoubtedly Peel's authority and parliamentary skills played an important part in this. The decision to omit the City of London from the proposal helped avoid the fate of Pitt's bill of 1785. Indeed, the general terms in which the bill was framed probably helped ease its passage, though it is still remarkable that Parliament was prepared to pass a bill that left unstated both the number and the distribution of the new police constables. Peel's ability would not have been sufficient in itself. Of greater importance was the change in sentiment within the ruling elites. The need for a strong police force to maintain order was now accepted across the political spectrum. Thus, on 19 June 1829 Peel's bill finally received the royal assent and by September of that year the Peelers appeared for the first time in Britain.

The development of policing in London has been studied in detail, not simply because of the traditional, if exaggerated, importance attached to 1829 but because it highlights the complexity of the motives behind reform. Contemporary concerns with the increase in crime were important. In this respect the orthodox interpretation has validity, even if its belief in an upsurge of crime is somewhat misplaced and does not give sufficient attention to increased expectations of security. Similarly, a belief that existing methods of law enforcement were inadequate was important, even if the orthodox view of the old watchmen is too much of a caricature. In an important sense, to use a phrase of Peel's, London had entirely outgrown its policing institutions by the late 1820s.[23]

However, there was more to the 1829 act than instituting more efficient means of crime fighting. Concerns about law enforcement, in the minds of Peel and others, ran beyond the parochial watchmen to the yeomanry and military. The threat of radicalism – not confined to London, as we shall see later – required a new form of control. To achieve this Peel was able to call on his Irish experience. In this respect the revisionist emphasis on the police as a means of stabilising a socially and politically volatile and divided nation has considerable force.[24] Peel's knowledge of policing in Ireland has a further significance. As well as knowing the structure of the Dublin police, Peel also had some knowledge of the nature of their work and this included attempts to control drunkenness and prostitution. It seems unlikely that Peel was unaware that a new police could be used to bring decorum as well as order to the streets of London.

Provincial England

Although London was seen as a special case, the debate about policing was not focused solely on the capital. It was increasingly clear that there was a nationwide problem that required urgent consideration. Both centrally and locally the question of policing aroused keen debate within elite circles. A variety of options was available and the breadth of discussions in the 1830s (and later the 1850s) gives the lie to the idea that police reform was a simple linear progression as the metropolitan model was brought to the rest of the country.[25] There was considerable support for traditional modes of policing in London. Unsurprisingly, similar attitudes were to be found in virtually all parts of provincial England. Fears of the threat to liberties posed by a centralising government, coupled with a not ill-founded belief that existing practices worked satisfactorily, meant that early proposals for major reforms in law enforcement received scant support, except in particularly prob-lematic areas such as Manchester or Merthyr Tydfil.[26] However, gradually, first among the national elite and later within the provincial elite, the realisation dawned that not only were existing practices inadequate but new proposals were less threatening than previously believed.

Contrary to earlier interpretations, it is now apparent that the Whigs were discussing the possibility of introducing a system of national policing in 1832. The recent discovery of a draft bill that would have effectively created 'a national network of police agencies responsible to the Home Office through the stipendiary magistrates' throws significant new light on the evolution of modern policing.[27] And yet, in certain respects, such a proposal should not be cause for great surprise. The idea of a national police force had been mooted by Peel in the debate on the Cheshire Constabulary Bill in 1829.[28] Moreover, given the known concerns in the 1820s about the efficacy of policing arrangements in many parts of northern England at a time of social and political instability, it is not entirely surprising that, in the aftermath of widespread rural disturbances (the Swing Riots of 1830/31) and the even more overtly political urban riots of 1831, in places such as Bristol, Derby and Nottingham, the government should be giving serious thought to improving the means of maintaining public order.

Nonetheless, a proposal that would have covered corporate and non-corporate towns as well as unions of towns or large rural districts was a dramatic step forward for a government that previously had said it would confine itself to improving the policing of the great towns.[29] Even more radical was the proposal to replace the 'great unpaid' justices of the peace, drawn from the ranks of gentlemanly volunteers, by stipendiaries. Even in the heightened atmosphere of 1832 it was by no means certain that such a measure could be carried in Parliament, despite the favour that it found with ministers. Melbourne, the Home Secretary in the Whig government led by Earl Grey, summed up the situation well: 'I do not myself think any measure short of this will be effectual, and for this, I fear the country is not yet prepared.'[30] This pessimism, combined with the more pressing realities of the Reform Bill crisis of May 1832, led to the dropping of the proposal. The idea did not die but the post-Reform Whig government saw Poor Law, rather than police, reform as the priority. However, the absence of legislation should not blind us to the importance of this proposal. Here was a clear indication of the Whigs' preferred solution to the problem of order. Furthermore, as the 1832 parliamentary debates reveal, there was a consensus of opinion among leading figures in both the government and the opposition that action was needed to make good the deficiencies in the apparatus for maintaining order in the country. There was still much to be done in determining a precise scheme and in making such a scheme acceptable to the provincial elites of England, but this does not detract from the significance of the advance that had been achieved within the national elite by the early 1830s.

Rural policing

Discussion of police reform in the early nineteenth century had been informed largely by the experience of London, and to a lesser extent the great towns, but the problems of law and order were not simply an urban phenomenon. From the 1790s onwards there had been sporadic disturbances in many parts of the countryside that had created localised concern.[31] Even more disturbing had been the Swing Riots, in which arson and machine breaking were the most public expressions of deep-rooted anger among rural labourers.[32] These disturbances had been dealt with by a traditional show of governmental force. Special assizes that handed out severe sentences were a clear demonstration of the government's determination to stamp out such insurrection. On the other hand, the ease with which the Swing troubles spread and the difficulties encountered by local magistrates in containing them raised very real doubts. A case could be made for a more effective local police force, if not to prevent such rioting, at least to contain it more effectively. The risk of a *Jacquerie* was not to be taken lightly by the rulers, local and national, of the country. By the 1840s, many rural districts, although no longer so disturbed as in 1830/31, were far from tranquil. Agricultural unionism and opposition to the new Poor Law, combined with more traditional forms of protest, such as arson, created a situation of continuing tension in many southern counties.[33] It is hardly surprising to find that the question of policing was a major source of debate and practical action in these years. Differing models of policing (and all that that implied in constitutional and financial terms) vied with one another. Different options were explored in a period of unprecedented experimentation, until the 1856 County and Borough Police Act brought things to a conclusion.

A consensus had emerged among members of the elite at Westminster in the early 1830s for some form of national policing scheme. The provincial elite, and in particular the rural elite, remained to be convinced. However, it would be wrong to suggest that this reflected a refusal to accept that there was a need for change. Although hard-line conservatives, arguing for the preservation of the status quo, never disappeared from the scene, their numbers were visibly declining in the 1830s. Rural society was changing and its rulers were only too well aware of the fact. A new approach was needed and, as Robert Storch has amply demonstrated, there was a flourishing provincial debate dating from the early 1820s onwards and a variety of new measures were put into practice in the 1830s.[34]

Three main approaches can be identified.[35] Perhaps the best-known was the adoption of the 1833 Lighting and Watching Act. This enabled vestries to appoint an inspector who, in turn, could appoint paid watchmen. It is impossible to say how extensively this act was used. It is clear, however, that in some districts it provided a useful way forward and, indeed, a way of avoiding establishing a rural police force after 1839.[36] The Norfolk parishes of Wymondham and Hingham, for example, took advantage of this legislation. Also organised under this act were the police of Croydon and Blackheath, both operating on the border of the Metropolitan Police district. The act was also adopted in several small towns such as Braintree, Walthamstow and Horncastle. In Horncastle, which had a population of 4,500 in 1841, the town's rate payers voted decisively in favour of establishing a police force under the provision of the act in 1838.[37]

A second model of policing was the so-called private subscription force. The best-known example was the Barnet Association, set up by Thomas Dimsdale. Initially two men watched a five-mile district around Barnet. Following the Swing Riots an increase in subscriptions led to the employment of six men. At Stow-on-the-Wold the gentry formed the Association for the Better Security of Life and Property, and employed two London policemen, under the control of three local justices, to patrol at night an area six miles in diameter from the centre of Stow. However, the contrast between privately and publicly paid policing should not be overdrawn. The police force at Blofield, Norfolk, started as a subscription force but eventually became a regular force under the 1833 act.

The third, though short-lived, model was derived from the working of the new Poor Law with its grouping of parishes into a single union. Indeed, it was rioting against the new Poor Law that led to the formation of such forces in certain parts of the country, such as Suffolk. Despite its popularity, particularly in parts of East Anglia, the practice of paying policemen from Poor Law rates was declared illegal in 1836.

It is important to note the degree of experimentation and the diversity of practice in the 1830s. There was not a consensus on the most appropriate form of rural policing. Options remained open and were not closed by the 1839 Rural Constabulary Act. However, before examining the genesis of this better-known piece of legislation, it is important to look at the motives that underpinned the experiments in policing that have just been detailed.

In several cases the development of a new mode of policing was a direct response by members of the local elite to a clear and large-scale threat to order. The Swing Riots were crucial formative events in parishes such as Stoke and Burnham in Buckinghamshire, as were the anti-Poor-Law disturbances in the Blything union in Suffolk and Swaffham in Norfolk. In a more general sense, considerations of social control played an important part. The Vicar of Tenbury, for example, speaking on behalf of 'the respectable part of the parishioners', was delighted that the 'idle and dissolute' were to be kept in check.[38] Similarly at Blofield in Norfolk the local justices were keen to have a police force that would supervise alehouses and, more generally, control the poor. However, the newer police were a response to ordinary crime; after all, there was a clear link between the older societies for the prosecution of felons[39] and some of the rural police of the 1830s. This is most clearly seen in the case of the subscription force at Stow-on-the-Wold, which was brought into being as a direct result of a brutal robbery and murder in 1834. However, the distinction between petty crime fighting and a more general surveillance of the poor was a fine one. The police of Wymondham and Hingham were intended to check theft, help implement the new Poor Law, as well as to keep an eye on the local alehouses. The attitude is well captured in the stated objectives of the Blackheath watch, namely, 'by a general and vigilant superintendence over the whole to note the conduct of the idle and suspicious and, by anticipatory and preventive measures to check the attempts of evil doers'.[40]

Local experimentation in new forms of policing provided an important element in the late-1830s debate. However, it must not be forgotten that the bulk of rural England was still under the unreformed parochial system. Moreover, such a situation was unsatisfactory not just to a zealous reformer such as Edwin Chadwick but also to many members of the ruling elite at Westminster, across much of the political spectrum, who had been concerned with the issue for most of the decade. Not surprisingly, especially after the introduction of the new Poor Law, the Whig government was turning its attention to the question of rural policing.

Chadwick was undoubtedly a driving force in the establishment of a royal commission on rural policing and in the writing of its report. However, it would be very misleading to see Chadwick as the main architect of the 1839 act and, indeed, to see the act as the embodiment of his wishes.[41] Russell, the Whig Home Secretary, was already actively considering police reform and had a plan of reform based on the ideas, not of the centralising moderniser Chadwick, but of the traditionalist Duke of Richmond. The appointment of the royal commissioners was a further blow to Chadwick. Colonel Rowan and Charles Shaw Lefevre, the first appointed, had little sympathy for Chadwick's centralising ideas. Indeed, Rowan was in contact with Richmond and made it clear that his ideas were largely the same.[42] The role of the 'great unpaid' was central and Chadwick was isolated from his fellow commissioners. Ultimately the report reflected more the interests of country gentlemen rather than the ideals of Benthamites.

Chadwick was also being outflanked as the report was being prepared. In February 1839 the Home Office sought the response of quarter sessions to a resolution that had been adopted in Shropshire advocating 'a body of constables appointed by the magistrates, paid out of the County rate' as the most desirable and efficient way forward.[43] Only half of the thirty-six quarter sessions to respond did so positively, but this was sufficient for Russell. When the bill was presented to Parliament it contained many of the royal commission's basic recommendations but there were crucial omissions. For Chadwick the outcome was a grave disappointment. The act (which did not deal with borough forces) that reached the statute book was permissive and contained little in the way of control by central government. The decision to appoint rural police forces was left in the hands of county magistrates. Furthermore, they would determine the size of the force, frame its rules and regulations, and appoint the chief constable.

The 1839 act has been presented by some historians[44] as a response to the perceived revolutionary threat of Chartism. Several leading figures, not least Sir Charles Napier, felt that the scale of popular disturbances revealed the need for efficient local police forces. Writing to the Home Office on 20 July 1839, he argued for 'the establishment of a strong rural police' for 'if the police force be not quickly increased we shall require troops from Ireland'.[45] The point, however, must not be overstated. There was concern with disturbances in parts of central and northern England. As Russell explained, 'many districts in the counties had in the present time come to be thickly peopled with a manufacturing or mining population, which partook of the character of a town population, while at the same time it was impossible to confer on them municipal institutions'.[46] This was a real, though not new, concern. However, ignoring problems of chronology,[47] it is clear that rural police reform was a well established topic of debate for many years previously. In many respects, the 1839 act is best considered as an addition to the range of policing options that had developed in the previous ten years or so.

The response to the government's initiative is interesting, if complex, as an analysis of the quarter sessions debates shows. Despite the suggestion that the debate in 1839/40 was about local versus central control, the evidence seems to point to a different conclusion: namely, that the real issues centred on who should exercise local control and what would be the financial and constitutional implications of reform. Adoption of the act was not uniform. The most reliable estimate suggests that thirty-five counties in England and Wales adopted the act (for part or all of the county) and, of these, twenty-four did so within the first two years of the act being passed.[48]

The pattern of adoption, however, is not clear cut. In some cases there is a link between recent disturbances and the creation of a police force. Several Lancashire magistrates, for example, made it clear that recent Chartist troubles had convinced them of the need for reform, though the fact that the initiative was taken by magistrates from the thinly populated and rural northern hundreds of Lonsdale North and Lonsdale South suggests that direct experience was not necessary. At the same time, magistrates in Staffordshire and the West Riding of Yorkshire decided not to adopt the act, notwithstanding the considerable disturbances they had experienced.[49] Proximity did not automatically lead to adoption. Indeed, the reverse may well have been true in some cases. Of a total of twenty-one English counties to adopt the act in 1839 and 1840, neither Bedfordshire, Cambridgeshire (Isle of Ely), Cumberland, Essex, Gloucestershire, Hampshire, Herefordshire, Hertfordshire, Norfolk, Northamptonshire, Suffolk (East), Sussex (East), Warwickshire, Wiltshire, nor Worcestershire could be seen as hotbeds of industrial unrest. Nor is there convincing evidence of a strong link between Swing disturbances and the adoption of rural police forces. Of the ten most riotous Swing counties, five adopted the act and five did not. The impact of anti-Poor-Law disturbances may have been greater, but of ten counties that experienced both Swing and anti-Poor-Law troubles five rejected the act, including the much-troubled counties of Kent and Berkshire. Such variations in response should not come as a complete surprise given what we now know of the variety of policing options available in the 1830s. Indeed, one might even expect to find a relationship between the innovative counties of the 1830s and the adopters of the 1839 act. Somewhat surprisingly, no clear pattern emerges. Among the innovative counties, Hampshire adopted the act while Kent did not, while among the non-innovative counties Wiltshire was keen to adopt while Somerset was not.[50]

In the absence of detailed local research it is not possible to give a totally satisfactory explanation of these variations. Nevertheless, cost was clearly an important consideration in non-adoption in certain districts, such as the West Riding of Yorkshire, Buckinghamshire and Lincolnshire. In Derbyshire the magistrates actually resolved to adopt the act but were forced to change their decision in the face of opposition from ratepayers.[51] Preventive policing, 'watching and suspecting', was seen to be too expensive and ran counter to a tradition of using the police, for example under the Special Constables Act, as an ad hoc response to specific problems. However, it would be simplistic to see opposition simply in financial terms, even when those financial considerations implied a model of policing. Equally important was the fear of centralisation. Opposition to Chadwick's proposals is well known and given exaggerated importance in police histories. When critics of the Rural Constabulary Act expressed their fears of centralisation they had in mind the demise of the individual justice with the removal of authority from petty sessions to quarter sessions, where, it was feared, the lord lieutenant and the larger landowners of the county held greater sway.[52] Finally, differing assessments of the threat to social order will have played a part in the decision-making process alongside ideological beliefs and pragmatic political consider-ations but the precise balance between these, and maybe other, factors remains a matter of speculation at present.

Although an important piece of legislation, the Rural Con-stabulary Act (and the amending act of 1840) was clearly not the last word in rural policing. Nor is it evident that there was a clear idea of progression at governmental level. Even if there was a vision at this level, important initiatives leading to legislation could emanate from below to strengthen the old system. The magistrates of Kent, not content with rejecting the 1839 act, were very active in making proposals to revivify the parochial constable system. Five such proposals were made between 1841 and 1852 and had a part to play in the evolution of the important, if often overlooked, Parish Constable Acts of 1842 and 1850. The 1842 act allowed for the payment of parish constables and sought to improve their quality by restricting their appointment to rate-payers, fit and of good character, aged between twenty-five and forty-five. Moreover, provision was made for the appointment of a paid superintending constable who, under the amending act of 1850, could be appointed for a petty sessional division of a county and who had responsibility for all parish constables and lock-ups. This system was adopted not only in Kent but also in Buckingham-shire, Dorset, Lincolnshire and Oxfordshire.

Thus, after some twenty years, or more, of discussion and experimentation rural England still exhibited a wide variety of

policing practices and, perhaps a little surprisingly, many parts of
the country still operated under an unreformed system. Where
change was taking place diversity was the order of the day. Despite
the fact that Melbourne had prepared a national police scheme in
the early 1830s, the evidence of the subsequent twenty years shows
a watering down of government intent, as reflected in the
permissive nature of the 1839 act, resulting from the limited
support for this piece of government legislation. In addition, a
variety of local initiatives, some of which – most notably those
from Kent and the subsequent legislation of 1842 and 1850 –
strengthened the old, parochial-based system of policing and quite
explicitly rejected any form of centralisation, be it regional or
national. Few could have anticipated that major change was only a
matter of years away. However, before looking at the advent of the
County and Borough Police Act, it is necessary to look at the
evolution of urban policing outside London.

Urban policing

The discussion of urban policing had focused almost exclusively
upon London from the second half of the eighteenth century.
However, by the early nineteenth century it was evident that the
rapidly growing towns and cities of central and northern England
were beginning to experience similar problems to those which
beset the capital. As metropolitan police reform was being
discussed in the mid and late 1820s many contemporaries were all
too aware that what was being proposed for London could easily
be extended to other towns and cities. As we have already seen, the
Whigs were discussing a scheme that would have covered the
whole country. The scheme would have allowed the government to
establish a police office and appoint a stipendiary magistrate with
the power to act as a justice of the peace for that town and its
surrounding county in any non-corporate towns with a population
of over 10,000 or in a corporate town in which the corporation
agreed, or a majority of ratepayers petitioned for, a new police.
Paid police constables were to be appointed by the stipendiary
magistrates, under the direction of the Home Secretary.[53]

However, nothing came of this scheme and no further action
was taken until 1835, when the Municipal Corporations Act was

passed. Clause 76, never debated nor amended, required borough councils to establish watch committees and to establish police forces. Melbourne, for whom this was very much a second-best option, made only a brief reference to policing powers towards the end of a very long speech and no reference whatsoever to crime as a major problem. Russell, similarly, referred only to his view of municipal government, which was 'that the keeping of the peace, or to use the words of the olden times, "the quietening of the towns", should be immediately under the control of the persons who are deemed proper to have government of that town.'[54] However, while it is important to see the policing proposals as part of a general concern with efficient municipal government, they cannot be divorced from the wider context of uncertain public order that had influenced discussion in the early 1830s.

The response to the 1835 act was patchy. Ninety-three out of 171 boroughs without a police force claimed to have taken action in the following two years. The inaccuracies of the figures relating to police strengths makes it impossible to give a precise picture of developments, but it is clear that there were some stark contrasts. In Liverpool, where the problem of a rapidly expanding port was exacerbated by large-scale immigration, a large police force was quickly established. Moreover, there was a conscious effort to break with past practices. The perceived weaknesses of the old system, which comprised a day force under the control of the town council, a night watch under the commission of watch, and a dock police under the dock committee, led to the recruitment in 1830 of a metropolitan policeman charged with the responsibility of reform. However, it was not until 1836 that the new Liverpool Police Force, under Chief Constable Whitty, was formed. Of the 360 men recruited to the force, less than one-third had served in the city's previous forces. By 1848 the number of men had risen to over 800. Manchester, incorporated in acrimonious circumstances in 1838, had a force of about 360 men by 1840, rising to about 450 by 1848. In Bristol, where there was a somewhat exceptional enthusiasm for police reform, a force of about 230 men was established in 1836. Birmingham, also incorporated in 1838, had a police force of only thirty men in 1839, though this had risen to over 300 by 1844, while Sheffield's force of 112 men was not established until 1848 and the new Leeds force, although established in 1836, was initially only twenty men, rising to 129 by the early 1840s. Further figures are given in Table 2.1.[55]

Even less change was to be seen among the medium-sized boroughs. Chester had a force of twenty-nine men for a population of 24,000, while Newcastle upon Tyne had eighty-nine men for its population of 70,000, and many of these were men who had been previously employed as watchmen. Some of the worst police: population ratios were to be found in Lancashire. Stockport had a force of thirteen men, a ratio of 1:3,806; Wigan six men, a ratio of 1:4,097; while Bolton had ten men, a ratio of 1:4,837. However, the worst situation of all was in Walsall, where three policemen operated at a ratio of 1:6,299. Most boroughs fell within these extremes, but ratios of 1:2,500 to 1:3,000 in places such as Chipping Norton, Helston and Tenby should not be allowed to obscure the fact that there was only one policeman in each of those towns.[56]

Generally speaking, adoption of the 1835 act was sporadic. As late as 1837 less than 55 per cent of boroughs had established police forces, though the figure had fallen to 20 per cent by 1842. Of the towns incorporated between 1835 and 1853, all nineteen set up police forces within two years of incorporation. Nonetheless, there is much force in Judith Hart's observation that the situation was 'nearer the world of early-nineteenth century watchmen earning a few shillings by casual police work than to the new world of professional, full-time, carefully recruited and supervised Metropolitan police officers.'[57]

It is almost impossible to give a satisfactory overview of borough policing in the period between the Municipal Corporations Act and the County and Borough Police Act of 1856. In 1839 43 per cent of boroughs were unable to provide figures, while 30 per cent were in the same position in 1848. Of those making returns in 1839, less than 30 per cent had desirable police: population ratios (that is, of 1:900 or better) while in 1848 the figure had fallen to below 20 per cent.[58] Once again, one is struck by the limited degree of progress, though this is not surprising given the almost total absence of central guidance and the limited transmission of ideas and best practices between provincial forces.

The policing provisions of the Municipal Corporations Act could provide only a partial answer to the problem of 'disorder'. The Reform Riots from 1829 to 1832 had demonstrated the scale and geographical spread of the problem. In addition to the well

Table 2.1. *Police numbers and police:population ratios, 1844*

Borough	Strength, including officers	Approximate population (1,000s)	Police:population ratio
Liverpool	715	300.0	1:420
Manchester	392	235.1	1:600
Birmingham	313	190.0	1:607
Leeds	140	150.6	1:1,076
Bristol	229	128.0	1:559
Newcastle	110	80.0	1:727
Bath	198	70.0	1:354
Salford	29	55.0	1:1,897
Leicester	51	48.2	1:945
Hull	105	41.6	1:396
Plymouth	39	36.5	1:936
Macclesfield	10	32.6	1:3,260
Coventry	17	30.0	1:1,765
Southampton	32	30.0	1:938
York	24	30.0	1:1,250
Worcester	26	27.0	1:1,038
Ipswich	15	26.1	1:1,740
Cambridge	30	24.5	1:817
Walsall	10	22.0	1:2,200
Whitehaven	13	20.0	1:1,538
Gloucester	17	18.0	1:1,059
Banbury	5	15.6	1:3,120
Canterbury	17	16.0	1:941
Lancaster	10	16.0	1:1,600
Lincoln	12	16.0	1:1,333
Bury St Edmunds	11	14.0	1:1,273
Taunton	16	14.0	1:875
Salisbury	12	11.5	1:958
Boston	12	12.9	1:1,075
Doncaster	13	11.0	1:846
Newcastle-under-Lyme	4	10.0	1:2,500
Poole	9	10.0	1:1,111
Scarborough	22	10.0	1:455
Truro	9	10.1	1:1,122
Louth	8	9.0	1:1,125
St Ives	9	8.0	1:889

Continued opposite

Stamford	13	7.8	1:600
Windsor	11	7.8	1:709
Newbury	8	6.5	1:813
Peterborough	11	6.1	1:555
Tavistock	4	6.0	1:1,500
Tewksbury	6	5.9	1:983
Hertford	6	5.5	1:917
Pontefract	6	4.8	1:800
Evesham	7	4.2	1:600
Maldon	7	4.0	1:571
Thetford	7	3.9	1:557
Dorchester	8	3.6	1:450
Blandford	5	3.3	1:660
Lyme Regis	4	2.5	1:625
Hereford	16	1.2	1:75

Source: *The Police and Constabulary List, 1844*, reprinted by the Police History Society, 1990.

known disturbances in Bristol, there were outbreaks of rioting in smaller market towns in the south-west, in Leicester, Nottingham and Derby as well as in Manchester, Bolton and Preston. It is hardly surprising that some senior Whigs considered far-reaching police reforms at this time. Nor is it surprising to find in cities like Bristol that the provision for policing in the Municipal Corporations Act was acted upon swiftly. However, such a response was not open to all. Moreover, popular radicalism remained a major problem, especially in certain northern industrial towns, such as Bolton, Bradford, Huddersfield, Oldham and Wakefield, in which condemnation of the new Poor Law had been added to the litany of complaint.[59] However, there were still powerful voices arguing against the introduction of new police. Major-General Bouverie, Commander of the Northern District, wrote at great length to the Home Office in August 1833 emphasising the disadvantages – inefficiency, expense and possible unconstitutionality – of using the new methods of control.[60]

Nonetheless, the problem of provincial disorder could not easily be contained by local police forces. Demands were made on the Metropolitan Police to send men to deal with short-term emergencies, though there was nothing to compare with the Peace

Preservation Police in Ireland.[61] In response to this provincial demand the government passed legislation in 1835 that allowed local magistrates to swear in Metropolitan policemen as special constables. Indeed, in the same year, Metropolitan Police Commissioner Mayne even went so far as to draft a bill for 'Providing Peelers "occasional" to distant places', though nothing came of this initiative following the fall of Peel.

However, it was with the upsurge of Chartism that urban policing reached crisis point in parts of England. In Manchester, Bolton and especially Birmingham there were major problems that revealed the inadequacies of local policing arrangements. In Birmingham the problem was compounded by fighting within the town's elite. This, as much as the threat of Chartism, seems to have swayed parliamentary opinion. It seemed safer to have the new police answerable to the Home Office rather than to a council dominated by liberal–radical sentiments.[62] The situation was exacerbated by the arrival of members of the Metropolitan Police.[63] Faced with the collapse of 'order' in three important provincial centres the government took urgent and extreme action. Government-controlled police, based on the London model, were proposed for a two-year period. Despite opposition to 'the French system of police' the proposals passed through Parliament and within three weeks had received the royal assent, in August 1839. By this tactic the third and fourth largest cities in the country were being treated in the same way as Dublin!

The coming of the 1856 County and Borough Police Act

Such measures were, however, intended to meet emergency conditions. There is little indication that significant new thinking was emerging in the 1840s. Indeed, the Town Police Clauses Act of 1847, which was intended to provide a pro forma for local acts, reinforced traditional thinking. However, as circumstances changed so too did thinking. Although seen as an 'age of equipoise', the 1850s saw a real and growing concern with maintaining order. The adequacy of borough policing came under increasing scrutiny, all the more so following the publicity surrounding inadequate policing during the riots in Stockport in

1852 and in Blackburn and Wigan in 1853.[64] A select committee report of 1853 gave a vivid description of lawlessness in the country and that December Palmerston, Home Secretary in Aberdeen's Peelite/Whig coalition, drafted a bill for 'establishing a General Police in England and Wales'. However, the proposals, especially that for the abolition of separate forces for boroughs and counties with small populations, met with considerable opposition. The following year, Palmerston was forced to withdraw the bill.

The events of 1854 were a major rebuttal for the government and yet within two years a police act was on the statute books. Two factors help explain this. First, the Crimean War, or more accurately fears of its aftermath, led to a rethinking on the state of policing. The thought of large numbers of unemployed, if not unemployable, ex-soldiers roaming the countryside re-awakened fears of a repeat of the disorders that had followed the ending of the Napoleonic Wars. There was no desire to repeat 1816. These fears were intensified by a further factor. The 1853 Penal Servitude Act ended transportation and introduced the ticket-of-leave system for releasing prisoners. The 'ticket-of-leave man' emerged as a bogey figure. The thought of another army, this time of ex-convicts, prowling the countryside led people to consider the benefits of compulsory policing. This issue, more than any other, provided justification for police reform in the debates of 1855 and 1856.

The 1856 County and Borough Police Act was a major piece of legislation for a number of reasons. While not a centralised scheme, the government was involved in the maintenance of efficiency through a system of annual inspections. Attached to this was a system of central funding. Efficient forces received a reimbursement of a quarter of the expenditure on police pay and clothing. Very small boroughs were omitted from the system of inspection and grant-in-aid. In addition, annual crime statistics were to be furnished to the Home Office. Finally, the act also marked a break with the traditional area of local government, that is, the parish, and divided the country in a way that matched perceived police needs. The act confirmed the tendency towards centralisation that spelt the end of parochial control, but it was centralisation at a county level rather than a national level that triumphed. However, as Steedman has forcefully argued, 1856 was a defeat for the boroughs. It was the 'provincial vision of the rural police as a kind of soldiery', with all that that implied, which triumphed.[65]

Opposition was still to be heard. Fears of the usurpation of local rights dominated a London meeting of mayors and councillors while the *Portsmouth Times* feared the introduction of 'a continental police in free England'.[66] In York both the *York Herald* and the *Yorkshire Gazette* found themselves in agreement. There was fear that the government was acting unconstitutionally and its proposals for police reform represented 'a base attempt upon the liberty of the subject and the privilege of local government'. The old cry of 'a standing army' threatening 'the darkest age of tyranny' was raised.[67]

Not all responses were negative. Several local newspapers supported the measure. This mood was summed up by the *Brighton Examiner*, which saw effective policing to be 'as necessary to the proper management of a town as gaslighting' and saw 'no danger to general freedom' in a centrally supervised police. Likewise, the *Norfolk Chronicle* was even more dismissive of old fears, seeing them as:

> anachronisms, mere hypothesis and exaggeration – more figures of speech got up to alarm timid Councillors and to make a 'telling' speech.... With our free institutions who has any fear of Austrian despotism or a military police finding favour here, except, indeed, it be a few political lecturing firebrands?[68]

More importantly, so did an increasing number of Members of Parliament. In the Commons the bill was passed by 259 votes to 106. County MPs, predictably, gave the bill considerable support but borough MPs also voted in favour, albeit by a majority of only eighty-three to sixty-nine. Equally striking was the fact that all parliamentary groups gave majority support. Even the Radical vote divided fifteen to twelve in favour.[69]

Conclusion

The County and Borough Police Act is rightly seen as laying the foundation of modern policing in England. It was the culmination of a long and tortuous process of reform. It is clear that the Whig interpretation, with its emphasis on the new police as the response to 'the golden age of gangsterdom' is, at best, a gross over-simplification. At worst it distorts our understanding of both the arguments for and against police reform. The law-abiding versus law-breaking model fails to take into account the socio-economic and political context in which police reform took place. To this extent the revisionist interpretation is correct to seek to place policing in a wider context. However, to characterise the police reform in terms of conflict between sectional and societal interests is also to oversimplify matters. Nonetheless, there is a sense in which this dichotomy provides a useful framework within which to analyse the development of police reforms. Public order considerations bulked large in the thinking of the propertied elite. Working-class 'mobs' that destroyed property in town and country, as much as working-class radicals who advocated the end of a property-based social and political order, had to be kept in control. The collapse of government in Birmingham was a brief but awful warning of what might happen.

However, there was more to the debates than a desire to protect the propertied against the threat, real or imaginary, of the propertyless. Increasingly advocates of police reform recognised the need for, and responsibility of, government to prevent as well as punish crime and to preserve order for the benefit of all classes. The demand for order was not confined simply to one class. The unspectacular benefits of policing to members of the working classes, as well as the middle classes, tempered opposition. In that respect, the traditional interpretation holds some validity. The fear that liberties were under threat diminished somewhat with time, though never entirely disappeared.

It is also an oversimplification to see the struggle for police reform in terms of a conflict between central and local government. Arch centralisers like Chadwick were in a very small minority and did not exert great influence on legislation. Nonetheless, there was a real conflict of beliefs between those who advocated control at a parochial level and those who wished to centralise at a county level. This was the real question at issue for much of the time and historians have all too often overlooked the validity and vitality with which the parish-based option was viewed in the second quarter of the nineteenth century. Ultimately, the problems and needs of an increasingly urbanised and industrialised society made the parish an inappropriate unit for policing, but this was by no means a foregone conclusion as late as the 1840s.

With the passing of the 1856 act a framework for policing the country had been established. However, the existence of legislation did not guarantee the creation of effective police forces. The practical problems were considerable and took time to solve. It is to this question that we now turn.

Notes

1   This interpretation was based on a migratory model of criminal behaviour and police reform, in which legislative change drove criminals from London to the major provincial cities and finally into the countryside to escape the clutches of the new police. Unfortunately, despite some support in certain sources, the facts do not support the case, as was demonstrated several years ago in J. Hart, 'Reform of the borough police, 1835–1856', *English Historical Review*, 70, 1955.

2   J. Styles, 'The emergence of the police: explaining police reform in eighteenth- and nineteenth-century England', *British Journal of Criminology*, 27, 1987.

3   Cited in J. Beattie, *Crime and the Courts in England, 1660–1800*, Oxford, Oxford University Press, 1986, p. 598.

4   V. A. C. Gatrell and T. Hadden, 'Nineteenth-century criminal statistics and their interpretation', in E. A. Wrigley, ed., *Nineteenth-Century Society*, Cambridge, Cambridge University Press, 1972; and D. Philips, *Crime and Authority in Victorian England*, London, Croom Helm, 1977.

5   P. King, 'Decision-makers and decision-making in the English criminal law, 1750–1800', *Historical Journal*, 27, 1984; and R. Paley, '"An imperfect, inadequate and wretched system?": policing London before Peel', *Criminal Justice History*, 10, 1989.

6   The fact that Peel chose to emphasise the crime statistics for London strongly suggests that fears of rising crime existed within his Westminster audience and could be exploited for the purpose of gaining support for police legislation.

7   References to men 'scarcely removed from idiocy' and 'contemptible, dissolute and drunken buffoons who shuffled along the darkened streets after sunset' are to be found in T. A. Critchley, *A History of Police in England and Wales*, London, Constable, 1978, pp. 18 and 30.

8   Paley, 'Imperfect, inadequate', *passim*.

9   V. A. C. Gatrell, 'Crime, authority and the policeman-state', in F. M. L. Thompson, ed., *Cambridge Social History*, vol. 3, Cambridge, Cambridge University Press, 1990, p. 248.

10 E. P. Thompson, *Customs in Common*, London, Penguin, 1991, especially chapters 4 and 5.

11 R. McGowan, 'A powerful sympathy: terror, the prison and humanitarian reform in early nineteenth-century Britain', *Journal of British Studies*, 25, 1986.

12 V. A. C. Gatrell, *The Hanging Tree: Execution and the English People, 1770–1868*, Oxford, Oxford University Press, 1994.

13 Styles, 'Emergence of the police', p. 21.

14 Lord Shelburne, *Parliamentary History*, xxi, 1780–81, col. 680, cited in D. Philips, 'A new engine of power and authority: the institutionalisation of law enforcement in England, 1780–1830', in V. Gatrell, B. Lenman and G. Parker, eds, *Crime and the Law*, London, Europa, 1980, p. 164.

15 Cited in Philips, 'New engine of power', p. 168.

16 *Ibid.*, p. 174.

17 Report of the Select Committee on the Police of the Metropolis, *Parliamentary Papers*, 1822 (440), iv, p. 11.

18 Philips, 'New engine', p. 181. See also Paley, 'Imperfect, inadequate'.

19 Cited in Philips, 'New engine', p. 183.

20 Almost half the soldiers in Britain were stationed in and around London. S. H. Palmer, *Police and Protest in England and Ireland, 1780–1850*, Cambridge, Cambridge University Press, 1988, p. 174.

21 *Ibid.*, p. 180.

22 *Ibid.*, pp. 291–2.

23 *Ibid.* Indeed, Peel referred to the country as a whole.

24 This comes close to Reiner's neo-Reithian position. However, the emphasis on the police as a means of control for the benefit of the ruling elite points more to a revisionist, class-based interpretation of the introduction of the Metropolitan Police.

25 The older histories and several more recent studies of local forces subscribe to the misleading metropolitan migration thesis.

26 Philips, 'New engine', p. 171.

27 D. Philips and R. D. Storch, 'Whigs and coppers: the Grey Ministry's national police scheme, 1832', *Historical Research*, 67, 1994, p. 80.

28 *Ibid.*, p. 77.

29 See especially Melbourne to Holland, *ibid.*, p. 79.

30 Melbourne to Grey, 17 March 1832, *ibid.*, p. 81.

31 A. Charlesworth, *An Atlas of Rural Protest in Britain, 1548–1900*, London, Croom Helm, 1983.

32 E. Hobsbawm and G. Rude, *Captain Swing*, London, Penguin, 1973.

33 Charlesworth, *Atlas*; and G. E. Mingay, ed., *The Unquiet Countryside*, London, Routledge, 1989.

34 R. D. Storch, 'Policing rural southern England before the police: opinions and practice, 1830–1856', in D. Hay and F. Synder, eds, *Policing and Prosecution in Britain, 1750–1850*, Oxford, Oxford University Press, 1989.

The earliest of these schemes was that of J. H. Warden, the constable of Bedfordshire, who proposed in the early 1820s the appointment of three permanent, paid officers who would supervise the parish constables. In turn, Bedfordshire would become, in this scheme, part of a national system.

35 Storch, 'Policing', p. 228.

36 C. Steedman, *Policing and the Victorian Community: The Formation of English Provincial Police Forces, 1856–80*, London, Routledge and Kegan Paul, 1984, p. 14.

37 B. J. Davey, *Lawless and Immoral: Policing a Country Town, 1838–1857*, Leicester, Leicester University Press, 1983, especially chapter 4; M. Scollan, *Sworn to Serve: Essex Police*, Chichester, Phillimore, 1993, p. 4.

38 Storch, 'Policing', p. 228.

39 The best-known is the Barnet Association.

40 Cited in Storch, 'Policing', p. 228.

41 A. Brundage, 'Ministers, magistrates and reform: the genesis of the Rural Constabulary Act of 1839', *Parliamentary History*, 5, 1986; D. Foster, *The Rural Constabulary Act, 1839*, London, Bedford Square Press, 1982; and Storch, 'Policing'.

42 Brundage, 'Ministers', p. 57.

43 *Ibid.*, p. 60.

44 F. C. Mather, *Public Order in the Age of the Chartists*, Connecticut, Greenwood Press, 1959; Palmer, *Police and Protest*.

45 Cited in Hart, 'Reform', p. 427.

46 Cited in Palmer, *Police and Protest*, p. 424.

47 Chartism did not become a major threat until well after the nature of the legislation had been agreed. Brundage, 'Ministers', p. 62.

48 Foster, *Rural Constabulary Act*, p. 19.

49 *Ibid.*, pp. 20–1. Staffordshire magistrates changed their minds following major disturbances in August 1842.

50 Storch, 'Policing', p. 252.

51 Foster, *Rural Constabulary Act*, p. 21.

52 Steedman, *Policing*, p. 19.

53 Philips and Storch, 'Whigs and coppers', p. 80.

54 Cited in D. Walls, 'The selection of chief constables in England and Wales, 1835–1985', unpublished MPhil thesis, University of York, 1989.

55 *The Police and Constabulary List, 1844*, Police History Society Monograph, no. 3, 1990, p. 51.

56 Palmer, *Police and Protest*, p. 400. In 1970 this ratio was less than 500:1.

57 Hart, 'Reform', p. 421.

58 *Ibid.*, p. 401. The 1856 Municipal Corporations Act referred, somewhat vaguely, to the appointment of 'a sufficient number of fit men'. The 1839 Rural Constabulary Act had specified a minimum of one policeman for every 1,000 population. This was not repealed by the 1856 act. The Home Office preferred a lower figure for the larger boroughs.

59 Oldham was particularly problematic. There had been bitter conflicts over control of the police, dating back to the early nineteenth century. Fear of 'Jacobinical constables' led the propertied classes to try a number of ruses to regain control. An 1826 Police Act created a town force run by a local police commission but, despite a property qualification, radical and trade unionist influence was felt. The propertied classes tried to use the 1839 Rural Constabulary Act to bring new police to the town but the outcome was a conflict which finally led to an open brawl between town and county policemen at a meeting of the petty sessions in 1847. The radical hold was broken later that year and in 1849 Oldham was incorporated and a force was established under the provisions of the Municipal Corporations Act. In nearby Rochdale a police act was passed in 1825 but there does not seem to have been the same degree of conflict. J. Foster, *Class Struggle and the Industrial Revolution*, London, Methuen, 1974, chapter 3; D. Taylor, *999 And All That*, Oldham, Oldham Corporation, 1968, chapters 2–4; and S. Waller, *Cuffs and Handcuffs: The Story of Rochdale Police through the Years*, Rochdale, Rochdale Corporation, 1957.

60 Palmer, *Police and Protest*, p. 408.

61 *Ibid.*, p. 409.

62 M. Weaver, 'The new science of policing: crime and the Birmingham Police Force, 1839–1842', *Albion*, 26, 1994.

63 Palmer, *Police and Protest*, pp. 416–17; and Weaver, 'New science'.

64 There were also riots in Hyde Park in 1855, though the response to police action was mixed.

65 Steedman, *Policing*, p. 27.

66 Palmer, *Police and Protest*, p. 510.

67 R. Swift, *Police Reform in Early Victorian York, 1835–1856*, York, University of York, Borthwick Papers, no. 73, 1988.

68 Palmer, *Police and Protest*, p. 514.

69 *Ibid.*

3

From 'blue locust' to 'bobby'?
The creation and development of
police forces, c. 1830–1914

We know they [the police] do their work well; most of us freely
recognize this. Foreign visitors speak in glowing terms of their virtues
and efficiency. (*The Times*, 24 December 1908, p. 7)

Introduction

The second quarter of the nineteenth century witnessed the 'birth
of the blues' but it was the second half of the century that saw the
creation and development of effective policing throughout the
country. The existence of a policed society is so often taken for
granted that the problems of turning theory into practice are easily
neglected. Nonetheless, despite major problems and in spite of
considerable temporal and regional variations, by 1914 a significant transformation had taken place. In little more than the reign of
Victoria, the country changed from being a society that was lightly
policed (if not unpoliced) and often 'rough' to one which was very
clearly policed and, for the most part, more 'respectable'.[1] As part
of this transformation the police themselves changed. A poorly
disciplined group of men, viewing policing as a stopgap occupation, having little sense of identity and little commitment to the
job, had been transformed into a well disciplined body, centred on
a clear and growing core of 'career' men, who had a clear view of
themselves as a quasi-professional group with a distinct role and
responsibility in society. Yet, despite the importance of this

44

development, comparatively little is known of the processes of change and less of the experience of the thousands of largely unknown men who comprised the various forces of Victorian and Edwardian England. It is these unsung figures who will be the main focus of this chapter.

The legislative changes of the 1820s and 1830s led to patchy and piecemeal developments but the 1856 act established a framework for the development of nationwide policing. Urban policing developed steadily after 1835, with the Municipal Corporations Act. The twenty or so forces of 1834 had risen to 130 by the early 1840s, at which level it remained until the 1856 act. By the mid-1870s up to 165 borough forces were in existence but subsequent amalgamations of small borough forces with county forces reduced the number to just below 130 in 1914. County forces were created later. Six were in existence in 1839 and only twenty-six by the early 1850s. Only after the passing of the 1856 County and Borough Act did every county in England and Wales have a force.

At the same time, the overall number of policemen increased as forces grew in size. In 1861 there was a total establishment of 20,488, which expanded to 54,314 by 1911. As a consequence the population per policeman fell from 980 to 664.[2] The Metropolitan Police Force was the largest in the country. Initially just over 800 strong, it had grown to over 5,500 by 1851. In comparison, the forces of Manchester and Liverpool in the late 1840s had 445 and 806 men, respectively.[3] By 1871 London's total was in excess of 9,000 policemen while on the eve of war in 1914 it was over 22,000. By that time London had one of the lowest population:police ratios, with 350 people to every one constable.[4]

Outside London the largest forces were the county forces, especially those of Lancashire and the West Riding, where numbers exceeded 1,000 by the early twentieth century. However, smaller counties, such as Essex with 465 men, had forces that numbered into the hundreds by 1914. Urban police forces varied considerably in size even in the late nineteenth century, when several smaller forces had been amalgamated. The larger cities, such as Liverpool and Manchester, had larger forces than many counties. The experience of Yorkshire provides a good example of the diversity to be found, as the figures in Table 3.1 demonstrate.

However, the process of growth was far less smooth than the basic figures would suggest. Turnover rates were extremely high,

Table 3.1. *The growth of selected Yorkshire police forces, 1856–1910*

	1856/ 60	1866/ 70	1876/ 80	1886/ 90	1896/ 1900	1906/ 10
West Riding	513	659	885	991	1,208	1,299
Sheffield	176	260	324	368	454	529
Leeds	208	281	354	420	454	629
Bradford	116	135	216	243	288	401
Halifax	34	57	72	77	98	114
Huddersfield	30	46	82	100	120	121
York	36	42	50	68	79	96
Pontefract	3	5	8	–	–	–
Ripon	2	2	4	–	–	–
Doncaster	–	12	20	24	31	40

–, forces not yet established or amalgamated with county forces.
Source: annual reports of Her Majesty's Inspectors of Constabulary.

especially in the early years. Some 3,400 men joined the Metropolitan Police in 1829/30 but only a quarter remained in post four years later.[5] High turnover rates were not confined to London. In Middlesbrough in the 1850s at least 30 per cent of recruits served less than one year and 55 per cent served less than five years. The real position was actually worse, as there was a further 28 per cent for whom the records of service were incomplete, but who were extremely unlikely to have served any length of time. In other words, it is not inconceivable that 60 per cent of the intake served less than one year and over 80 per cent less than five years.[6]

Nor was the problem unique to urban forces. Of recruits to the Buckinghamshire force in 1857, 47 per cent served less than one year while the comparable figure for Staffordshire in 1856 was 46 per cent.[7] The situation was almost as bad in Lancashire. Between 1845 and 1860 just over 40 per cent of recruits served for less than one year.[8] Such figures meant, not surprisingly, that annual turnover rates (that is, the number leaving as a percentage of the total force) were high. As late as 1865 the annual turnover rate in the Metropolitan Police was 13.5 per cent, though by the mid-1880s this figure had fallen to about 5 per cent.[9] In contrast the overall turnover rate for England and Wales stood at just under 14 per cent and did not fall below 10 per cent until the mid-1880s.[10] The national figures conceal two important contrasts: first between borough and county forces – men left the former in higher numbers than the latter; second between north and south – between 1856 and 1880 the turnover rate in the counties was halved but in the south the fall was from 15 to 8 per cent whereas in the north it was from 30 to 15 per cent.[11] As one somewhat dispirited chief constable told the Select Committee on Police Superannuation Funds in 1875, 'If the men stay two years, there is some hope of them staying longer, but the vast proportion of men change within the year, or the first few months'.[12]

Becoming a policeman

To explain these high turnover rates we must look at the men who became policemen, their backgrounds, their reasons for joining, their attitude towards policing as an occupation and the nature of the job. In the eyes of many chief constables and recruiting sergeants, the ideal recruit was an agricultural labourer. He was seen to have both the necessary physical strength and the appropriate mental qualities of stoicism and deference to become a loyal servant upholding the rule of law and maintaining social order and stability. The image of ploughman turned policeman, which was central to the model of policing that triumphed in 1856, also became well established in popular culture in the nineteenth century. The reality was somewhat different. Recruitment patterns were more diverse and agricultural labourers did not necessarily make the best policemen. For example, of nineteen men who had been awarded a pension in the Buckinghamshire force, recruited in four selected years in the 1860s and 1870s, only four were from this background. Of the other nine agricultural labourers recruited in these years, four were dismissed and five resigned, all after relatively short periods of service.[13]

Nonetheless, it is quite clear that agricultural labourers were an important source of recruits for many forces. Bristol was not alone in recruiting many of its men from the surrounding countryside. County forces drew from a similar pool. But their importance in the overall composition of police forces is easily overstated. Labourers constituted about 50 per cent of the recruits to the Buckinghamshire and slightly less of the men joining the Staffordshire force in the

1860s.[14] The remainder were drawn from several occupations. In Buckinghamshire, grooms, blacksmiths, thatchers, wheelwrights, carpenters and bakers became policemen. In Staffordshire, miners, shoemakers, brickmakers, moulders, puddlers, potters, engine drivers and even a printer joined the force. Lancashire constables in the years between 1845 and 1870 were drawn from a wide range of occupations: 38 per cent of recruits had been labourers (and not all of these would have been rural workers) while fifty-four different skilled occupations were to be found. Boot- and shoemakers, carpenters, joiners, cabinetmakers, and so forth became policemen. The textile industries also provided a substantial number of recruits.[15]

A broader analysis of the occupational background of police recruits from 1840 to 1900 confirms this picture of diverse recruitment, as Table 3.2 shows. Three points deserve to be made about these figures. First, and predictably, a substantial percentage of police recruits were designated as labourers of one sort or another. Second, notwithstanding the shrinkage of the agricultural sector, especially after 1870, agricultural labourers constitute an over-represented group among police recruits. Finally, these observations need to be qualified by the fact that a large minority of men were drawn from a wide range of occupations other than labouring.

Police recruits, whatever their occupational background, tended to be younger, single men. In 1863 70 per cent of Buckinghamshire recruits and 96 per cent of Staffordshire recruits were unmarried.[16]

Table 3.2. *Occupations of police recruits, 1840–1900*

Force	Labourers	Agricultural work	Traditional trades	All others
Metropolitan	36	11	15	38
Birkenhead	39	13	5	43
Hull	60	4	10	26
Ipswich	38	7	13	42
East Suffolk	48	18	6	28
Worcestershire	35	18	14	33

Adapted from C. Emsley, *The English Police*, 1991, p. 181.

Metropolitan Police recruits in early Victorian England were allowed to have a family of three children but by the end of the century this figure had been reduced to two.[17] Many forces quite explicitly stated in their recruiting campaigns that married men need not apply.[18] Only in exceptional circumstances were men aged over thirty-five to be recruited to the police. Few forces had a lower age limit for recruits but most men seem to have joined in their twenties, that is, having already experienced work in one form or another.[19] The mean age of Lancashire new recruits between 1845 and 1870 was twenty-six years but there was a decline from twenty-eight years to twenty-five years between 1845/50 and 1866/70.[20] In the Metropolitan Police the mean age of recruits fell from twenty-six in 1833 to twenty-four in 1850 and reaching twenty-two and a half by the turn of the century.[21]

Why did men become policemen and how did they view their new occupation? For many early Victorians, policing was a new and low-status occupation. Few men became policemen for positive reasons. Agricultural labourers particularly, and unskilled men generally, joined to escape low wages and irregular earnings. The chairman of the Bristol watch committee was quite explicit: 'Our recruits all come from districts where work is bad and wages light ... a large number of them [Bristol policemen] come from the lower parts of Somersetshire and Devonshire, where wages are notoriously considerably below the average'.[22] Major Ashton Warner, Chief Constable of Bedfordshire, told the 1875 Select Committee on Superannuation Funds that wages in his force were some 5s (25p) a week better than the average wage in the district.[23] The importance of economic considerations was emphasised by Robert Titchman, the Head Constable of the Norwich Police Force. In his opinion, 'a police constable would rather obtain agricultural employment if he got a shilling a week more, than remain a constable at 22s'.[24] Geographical patterns of recruitment provide a sensitive guide to the distribution of poverty in the catchment areas of the various forces.

Some skilled men donned the uniform having joined the ranks of the technologically unemployed. In 1866 the Stafford boot and shoe trade was in severe decline and in that year six shoemakers, five locally born, joined the Staffordshire force while chairmakers and french polishers joined the Buckinghamshire force in the early 1870s as the local furniture industry was in decline.[25] Others joined as a means of tiding over a downturn in the local economy. The sharply fluctuating fortunes of the iron and steel industry in Middlesbrough had a clear impact on recruitment into the local police force. As Isaac Wilson, the long-serving chairman of the town watch committee, conceded, it was 'simply a question of wages'.[26] As industrial wages fell it became easier to recruit and retain men but as wages rose problems increased for the local force.

Yet others signed on for opportunist reasons. Becoming a policeman was one way of effecting a move to a town, a temporary phase, a bridge to a better job. Trained ex-policemen with good references became more employable in a range of occupations. As the Head Constable of Sheffield ruefully observed of certain recruits, 'when they have been drilled and smartened up, there is a great demand for them as porters, timekeepers and so on.'[27] And for some it was no more than a means of moving back home, like the Aylesbury-born blacksmith who, having worked in Ontario for several years, came home via the Buckinghamshire Police Force, in which he served for less than six months.[28]

For good reason, it has been argued that 'temporary desperation' was a major motive for becoming a policeman in forces that 'dealt in failures and casualties'.[29] However, this negative picture has to be put into perspective. In a rapidly changing economy, with many lowly paid occupations, policing, with its security of employment, regularity of pay and a variety of fringe benefits, could be seen in more positive terms and the steady flow of recruits can be seen as a measure, albeit crude, of its underlying attraction as a source of employment. Moreover, not all recruits came from poorly paid and/or declining industries. Almost 30 per cent of the recruits joining the Lancashire constabulary came from occupations that paid more than the police and a further 8 per cent from occupations with comparable wage levels. But for some recruits the material advantages were part of a wider attraction. It was not simply the pay but 'the prospect, the promotion by merit, the recognition of faithful service, the appreciation of moral character,' as well as the pension for old age.[30]

The negative reasons for joining played an important part in the high turnover rates experienced by the early police forces. However, other factors played their part. Becoming a policeman, as opposed simply to joining the force, was no easy matter. The demands of the job, both physical and mental, were considerable; the standard of behaviour that was expected, not just on duty but also off, demanded a high degree of self-discipline, while the restrictions on the lives of family members and the isolation from the mainstream of working-class society could easily become too much for many men. The high level of departures can be seen as a measure of the cumulative dissatisfaction among policemen, and not all newly recruited, with their occupation.

Recruits were often thrown straight into police work with little or no training beyond basic drilling. The skills involved in policing were, for the most part, acquired on the job. Exceptionally, the first recruits to the Hull Police Force in 1836 received some rudimentary training from Superintendent MacManus, but the practice fell into disuse and was not revived until 1883.[31] There is little evidence of new men receiving any training until the late nineteenth century. It seems to have been more common to send out new recruits with a more experienced man. In this way knowledge and experience would be passed on. This may have been considered satisfactory in the third quarter of the nineteenth century but, perhaps significantly, there was a move towards more formal training in the last decades of the century. In the 1880s 'systematic instruction in police duties is given to recruits' to the Metropolitan Police through classes run by Captain Knollys at Kensington. After three weeks recruits were posted to their divisions.[32] More rigorous training came with the opening of Peel House as a training school in 1907. It is difficult to be precise about the situation in the provinces but, in addition to the revival of training in Hull in the 1880s, members of the Norfolk county constabulary received a course in police duties in the late 1890s while in the early 1900s members of the Essex police were expected to undertake a month's training at headquarters in Chelmsford, where they studied police law and procedure as well as undergoing drill. In the East Riding constabulary, constables were instructed to study *The Police Manual* for half an hour a day in 1907. There were also educational classes and examinations, such as those introduced at the same time by Norman Riches for the Middlesbrough force, intended particularly for those wishing to become first-class constables or sergeants.[33]

Working the beat was at the heart of police work in town and country. Long hours were spent, in all weathers, tramping the streets and lanes of the nation. Much of this work could be highly tedious and conducted in isolation, especially in the countryside. For the heavily uniformed officer on the beat, adverse weather conditions – and the extreme heat of a summer's day could be as demanding and demoralising as the wet of a winter's night – added to the difficulties, bringing both short-term discomfort and longer-term ill-health. Self-discipline was a cardinal virtue for, in addition, there were obvious temptations to which many succumbed. Snatching a brief nap, taking a quick drink or falsifying entries were common disciplinary offences.[34]

The hours spent on duty were long, even by contemporary standards. In several cases men worked fourteen hours a day, seven days a week. Exceptionally, as late as 1865, the police in Stratford-upon-Avon worked a fifteen-hour day. More typically, Bedfordshire policemen in the mid-nineteenth century worked ten- to twelve-hour shifts, during which time they would patrol on foot up to twenty miles a day. Not all forces worked such long hours. In 1872 the Bristol watch committee reduced the hours of duty from ten to eight hours per day. The Norwich force, from its inception in 1836, worked a system of seven- to nine-hour shifts. The night shift patrolled the suburbs in pairs from 11 p.m. to 6 a.m., the early day shift continued patrolling the suburbs in pairs from 6 a.m. to 8 a.m., at which time until 2 p.m. they patrolled the city singly. Finally, there was a further day shift, patrolling singly the city from 2 p.m. to 11 p.m. York was similar. Initially a two-shift system had been worked which involved policemen being 'exposed to the severest weather' for over nine hours in summer and ten in winter. In 1845 a new system of three nine-hour shifts was introduced. Day duty ran from 9 a.m. to 6 p.m., evening duty from 6 p.m. to 3 a.m., and night duty from 9 p.m. to 6 a.m. The shifts were changed in 1850. The day shift now ran from 7 a.m. to 10 p.m., the evening shift from 5 p.m. to 3 a.m., and the night shift from 10 p.m. to 7 a.m. Despite a petition from the police which brought a brief reduction in hours, long hours remained the norm. Indeed, in 1855 it was reported that there was a two-shift system in operation, comprising a day shift from 6 a.m. to 6 p.m. and a night shift from 9 p.m. to 6 a.m. However, even where shorter hours were worked, split shifts were a source of discontent. It is difficult to translate this information into the lived experience of the individual policeman because of the absence of evidence. However, the pocketbook of one Norfolk constable reveals that, between February 1845 and

August 1846, he had only two days off and these were to attend his mother's funeral.[35]

Gradually hours were standardised across the country. By the mid-1870s a shorter shift of eight hours per day in the north and nine hours a day in the south had become common, but variations still persisted. Conditions improved in the latter part of the nineteenth century as rest days and holiday entitlement were recognised but the policeman was not one of the more favoured members of a society in which leisure time was becoming more common and more important. Moreover, the policeman was expected to be available for duty at all times. Some were not allowed to leave town without permission. Chief Constable Bower, of the East Riding constabulary, refused to grant holidays to his men if they stayed at home idle! Even when away from their home town he expected them to report to the local station to indicate availability in case of emergency.[36]

Despite the loneliness of much beat work, policing took place in a closely regulated hierarchy. The ordinary constable was made very aware of his position both within the force and within society as a whole. He was expected to exercise self-discipline and follow codes of behaviour, on and off duty, that were not part of normal working-class culture. Intended, in part at least, to be an agent of social discipline, the policeman was also subject to rigorous control by his superiors. He was expected not to drink, not to gamble, nor to smoke in public. Attendance at fairs or race meetings was also forbidden. Insofar as he appeared in the public house or at the racecourse he did so as a policeman, responsible for the enforcement of a code of behaviour that was not readily accepted by many members of the working classes. He was to be the embodiment of the social discipline that many of his masters wished to see imposed throughout society. In addition, the policeman was expected to conduct himself in exemplary fashion in his private life. Debt was to be avoided, wives were to be maintained, and religion was to be properly observed. As late as 1898 a standing order instructed all Watford policemen to attend divine service once on Sunday. Married men accompanied by wives and children were allowed to attend in plain clothes but men attending alone were to attend in uniform. Nor was this unusual. From Buckinghamshire in the 1850s to Shropshire in the 1890s, county policemen were instructed to attend church in full dress, while similar instructions were given to borough forces from Luton to Hull.[37]

Even personal appearances were subject to close scrutiny. Short hair, regular monthly haircuts and trimmed beards were commonly specified. Watford policemen were given very precise instructions. Non-shavers had to have a full set of beard and moustache. Shavers, however, had more options. They could grow a moustache or they might wear a moustache and whiskers. However, in the latter case, 'the whiskers must be cut short, and must not come lower than on a level with the mouth,' while there had to be 'the space of an inch between the whiskers and the moustache'![38] In Monmouth beards were not to be longer than two inches. Others were less fortunate. Until 1873 whiskers were compulsory in the Maidstone borough force. The reverse applied in the East Riding force. Initially, beards had been forbidden but in 1872 the privilege of growing a beard and moustache was granted.

Other restrictions could be imposed. Uniforms had to be worn even when off duty in the early years. Robert Bruce, Chief Constable of Lancashire from 1868 to 1876, felt it necessary to issue a general order informing his men that 'a shooting jacket and wide awake hat is not the dress in which they should appear in public, and more especially when visiting … such towns as Liverpool and Manchester'.[39] It was only in 1890 that the men of the East Riding force were permitted to wear plain clothes when not on duty. Most county forces insisted on 'approving' prospective spouses and requiring that they should not work, though borough forces appear to have adopted a more liberal stance. One force refused to allow a constable to marry without signing a declaration stating that he was free of debt and owned either £20 of furniture or possessed £20 in cash. Domestic respectability was expected. Somewhat harshly, the unfortunate PC George Stewart of the Essex police was requested to resign in 1859, 'his wife being insane'. The drive for respectability even extended, in some forces, to restrictions on the keeping of dogs, pigs and fowl.[40]

Lastly, the isolation of the policeman and his family should be stressed. The policeman was recruited from the working classes, and his job was to police that very section of the population. As we shall see in more detail in the next chapter, policing often involved the enforcement of codes of behaviour that were seen by sections of the working classes as alien and was seen to impinge upon the time-honoured customs of street leisure or the street economy. This sense of difference was accentuated by the lifestyle, the embodiment of respectability, that was expected of the policeman. Never off duty, never truly one of the community, he lived in but was not part of working-class life. Furthermore, his family could not escape the fact that they were the constable's wife and children. The solitary constable in Flora Thompson's Candleford Green was described as 'a kindly and good-tempered man' but despite this 'nobody seemed to like him, and he and his wife led a somewhat isolated life, in the village but not entirely of the village' — a point also made by Richard Jervis when describing early policing in Lancashire.[41] Isolation was compounded by the constant moving that took policemen and their families from one posting to another. A constable could expect to move several times, especially in the early stage of his job. Alfred Jewitt of the East Riding constabulary moved station nine times in a career spanning twenty-eight years, while Richard Hann, during his twenty-seven years, served in thirteen different places in Dorset. His longest stay, four and a half years in Sixpenny Handley, was his tenth posting.[42]

Leaving the force: resignations and dismissals

In view of this closely regulated and isolated life of the policeman, it is hardly surprising to find that many men either left of their own accord or were dismissed (Table 3.3). The former was a reflection of the individual's dissatisfaction with the force and became the increasingly important reason for leaving as length of service increased; the latter was a reflection of the force's dissatisfaction with the individual and was most important as a cause of leaving in the first year of service.

The impact of dismissals changed dramatically. In the early years of certain forces the number of dismissals was extremely high. In the first year of the East Riding constabulary, for example, there were forty-two dismissals, the equivalent of the full establishment. However, over time, dismissals declined in importance as a cause for termination of service. In the Lancashire force the percentage of men dismissed fell from 37 per cent to 18 per cent between 1845/50 and 1866/70. During the same period the percentage of terminations due to resignations rose from 51 per

Table 3.3. *Reasons for leaving the police: selected forces, 1856–1880 (as a percentage of men leaving in year)*

	1856	1863	1866	1876	1880
Under one year's service					
Resignation					
Staffordshire	47	49	46	46	55
Buckinghamshire	46	75	63	33	43
Dismissal					
Staffordshire	53	51	50	54	45
Buckinghamshire	53	25	36	67	57
One to two years' service					
Resignation					
Staffordshire	68	50	50	48	80
Buckinghamshire	43	75	83	50	66
Dismissal					
Staffordshire	31	48	44	52	20
Buckinghamshire	56	25	17	50	33
Two to five years' service					
Resignation					
Staffordshire	70	76	64	38	57
Buckinghamshire	76	0	80	100	100
Dismissal					
Staffordshire	29	8	29	62	43
Buckinghamshire	24	100	20	0	0
Over five years' service					
Resignation					
Staffordshire	46	26	38	32	15
Buckinghamshire	24	57	30	17	25
Dismissal					
Staffordshire	13	7	15	13	9
Buckinghamshire	6	0	0	0	0

These figures do not always total 100 per cent because some men died in service and others were pensioned off.

Adapted from C. Steedman, *Policing the Victorian Community: The Formation of English Provincial Police Forces, 1856–80*, 1984, pp. 95–6.

cent to 62 per cent. In the Met in the 1880s dismissals accounted for just under 30 per cent of intake but by the early twentieth century the figure had fallen to 6 per cent.[43]

Explaining why men resigned is not easy. Reasons were not usually recorded. However, scattered entries in constables' conduct books and the evidence given, for example, to the 1875 Select Committee on Police Superannuation Funds, suggest that better pay and less arduous work conditions were the dominant factors. PC John Turner left the Middlesbrough force in 1866 to become a timekeeper in the local iron works, a job that almost certainly brought him higher pay, though the same could not be said of William Gibbon, who left to become a gardener in the town's Albert Park. Nonetheless, pay was the more commonly given explanation, work conditions probably the more important. Others left for more personal reasons: some to tend sick relatives, like William Jones, who left Middlesbrough to return home to Byker to support his widowed mother; others because they or their spouses wished to return home. However, the overwhelming impression is that the vast majority of men who resigned did so because the job was too demanding either for the current rate of pay or at any price. The individual's dissatisfaction with the force was couched largely in financial terms: too much was asked for too little reward.

In contrast, the reasons that led men to be dismissed are well recorded. The main ones were drunkenness, neglect of duty, insubordination and a more general failure to act in the manner expected of a constable. The most common reason given for dismissal was undoubtedly drunkenness. In town and country policemen succumbed in their hundreds to the lure of hard liquor. The first Metropolitan Police Commissioners, Rowan and Mayne, had to confess that 80 per cent of dismissals were due to drink. Other forces suffered, though perhaps not to the same extent. The reasons are not difficult to find. The temptation to take a quick drink while working a beat in the cold and wind-swept streets of Middlesbrough in the winter or while tramping the dusty lanes of Norfolk during a hot summer are easy to appreciate. But the folly of some men is less comprehensible. Constable Hodges of the Dorset constabulary was dismissed in July 1857, having spent 'several hours in a Public House at Iwerne and playing skittles, whilst there he had his pockets picked of his handcuffs by one of his companions,' while Constable Collins could not have been surprised at the decision to dismiss him after he had regaled his prisoner with strong drink at several hostelries, including the Green Dragon Inn at Piddletrenthide.[44] Drunkenness was a problem associated with the lower ranks, but not all officers were paragons of virtue.

Drinking was often linked with neglect of duty. Constable Audus, one of Hull's earliest and least successful policemen, was dismissed for being drunk and incapable on his beat on his first day of duty. This was exceptional but large numbers of recruits succumbed to the temptation of drink in the early weeks and months after recruitment. Others combined neglect of duty with insubordination and even physical assaults on senior officers. Thomas Taylor and Jewitt Hardy were dismissed from the Middlesbrough force in the mid-1860s for assaulting a sergeant, but Harry Bickley took things a stage further by verbally abusing an inspector and destroying property in his office. John Bottomley was likewise dismissed from the Oldham force for attempting to strike the Chief Constable.[45]

Sexual misconduct was the downfall of many men. Frequenting brothels and committing adultery (or perhaps more accurately being discovered doing such things) often led to dismissal. Constables Caddy, Metcalf and Robinson were all dismissed in 1888 for having been discovered in a Middlesbrough brothel at 2 a.m. on a Sunday morning, while Constables Blakeborough and Nash lost their jobs as the result of 'highly improper conduct', that is, being married men but keeping the company of a widow and a young lady, respectively. But this was nothing when compared with one member of the Worcestershire constabulary who was dismissed after 'having intercourse ... with a girl on two occasions on Sunday afternoon April 18th. 1880, in full uniform and broad daylight'. The offence was compounded by the fact that this 'conquest' was witnessed by two men and several children. But he was not alone in courting disaster. Constable Cook of the West Suffolk Rural Police not only allowed a prostitute to stay in his room at Mildenhall Police Station but left his keys with her when he went on duty while his colleague Constable Dawson indulged in repeated acts of adultery with the wife of a convicted felon. More foolhardy was James Brook, a constable whose career with the Oldham police was short lived. In the space of one week he was disciplined for misbehaving with a married lady, being found asleep on duty and finally, in an act that led to his dismissal, 'taking indecent liberties with the daughter of Inspector Winterbottom'.[46]

Men were dismissed for a variety of other reasons but many, if not all, had some bearing on the respectability of the man concerned. Two who failed to meet the standards of the day in Oldham were dismissed for 'eating tripe at a market stall'; another was Constable Davis of the Essex force, who was dismissed in 1858, having been 'found covered in vermin', but Constable Marchbanks' dismissal, three years earlier for being 'connected with Mormons', is less clear cut.[47] In one sense the pattern of dismissals reveals a determination to remove men who were not giving value for money but, in a more profound sense, the force's dissatisfaction with the individual, as expressed through dismissals, was more a moral judgement on the character of the individual officer.

Discussions of discipline and dismissal concentrate on the lower ranks, and with good reason. The quality of many early recruits was poor indeed, and this created great difficulties for those seeking to build an effective force. This was particularly true of the smaller boroughs. The new police in Sudbury were a grossly unsuccessful body. In the worst cases, such as Ipswich in August 1842, the force was dismissed *en masse*. However, such a wholesale clear-out highlights an otherwise neglected point, that is, the inadequacies of many senior officers at this time. For example, in 1845 the Head Constable of the Bury St Edmunds force was dismissed for drunkenness, while Superintendent William Baxter of the Shropshire constabulary was dismissed for embezzlement in 1850.[48]

Even greater problems were experienced by the newly formed East Riding constabulary in the 1860s and 1870s. Despite repeated exhortation from the Chief Constable, Major Layard, there were persistent problems with the superintendents in the force. Superintendent Green, fined 15*s* for laughing and joking with members of the Rifle Corp and 'making water with his men outside the house of Dr. Watkins' hardly set a good example but was not one of the worst offenders in the senior ranks. Superintendent Ward was found guilty of gross carelessness and bad book-keeping. Superintendent Lazenby, already in disgrace for being improperly dressed on parade, having rusty spurs and mould on his weights and measures, was fined £2 3s in 1871 for employing constables to dig his garden when they should have been on duty. The first Deputy Chief Constable, Superintendent Gibson, was demoted to the rank of sergeant, having been found guilty of a gross case of drunkenness, neglect of duty and absconding from the force. However, the most spectacular miscreant was Superintendent Joseph 'Jack the Lad' Young, who retired on an annual pension of £40 in 1872. In an eventful career he was found guilty, *inter alia*, of drunkenness, withholding information, falsifying divisional accounts, forging the signature of a police constable on three separate occasions, loaning out his police horse to two local publicans and, in a further gesture perhaps intended to improve relations with the local community, helping out in his son's butcher's shop, cleaning game, dressing meat and serving customers, while in police uniform.[49]

Finally, it is necessary to look at the changing balance between resignations and dismissals. There are two different elements to be considered. The first concerns variations between ranks and length of service, the second variations over time.

As one might expect, dismissals were most common and relatively more important among newly appointed men in the lower ranks. Roughly a half of all dismissals fell into this category.[50] Thereafter, the likelihood of dismissal falls dramatically. However, it would be misleading to assume that once a man had served two or three years he had successfully internalised police discipline and was unlikely to be found guilty of ill-conduct. Clearly, a small minority of longer-serving men of all ranks were dismissed, but the overall figures obscure a particular problem for those who failed to achieve promotion and for whom the frustrations of the job led to misconduct and dismissal.

Resignations were also highest among newly appointed men in the lower ranks. Slightly less than a half of all resignations took place within the first year of appointment. The numbers fell of sharply thereafter but not so sharply as the number of dismissals. As a consequence, resignation (that is, individual dissatisfaction with the police) became relatively more important as a cause of leaving the force in the first ten years of service. This suggests that it was easier, or took less time, for a police force to bring a man up to an acceptable standard than it was for an individual to adjust to the demands of policing.

The second change that emerges from the figures is the declining importance over time of dismissals as a reason for termination of service. A number of reasons may be given for this. In part, it might be due to a lowering of disciplinary standards. Certainly there is evidence that the Metropolitan Police took a tougher stance in the early Victorian years and gradually relaxed standards during the latter part of the century.[51] In part it might be due to an improvement in the quality of applicants. The labour force of the late nineteenth century, taken as a whole, was more disciplined and self-disciplined than its early-Victorian counterpart. Furthermore, the decision to become a policeman became less opportunistic as the economy developed after the very difficult years of the 1830s and 1840s, and the demand for labour soaked up large numbers of unskilled men. It may also be the case that the decision became less ill-informed as police forces developed and more men had, or knew those who had, experience of police work.

The emergence of the long-term policeman

The problem of stubbornly persistent high turnover rates worried many senior police officers in the mid-nineteenth century. In addition, many men who managed to remain in the force had not entirely acquired the self-discipline expected of a constable. However, gradually, important changes did take place. In particular, as can be seen from detailed analysis of the composition of individual forces, there emerged the 'career policeman', that is, the long-serving man who went on to receive a pension (Table 3.4).

Not all of these men will have joined with the intention of becoming career policemen. After joining out of necessity, many will have stayed out of necessity. However, others did join for more positive reasons, often following fathers or other relatives.[52]

Most analyses of police forces have concentrated on the third quarter of the nineteenth century but the growing maturation and consolidation are more clearly seen when the analysis is extended to the early twentieth century. This can be seen in the case of the initially small, but rapidly expanding, borough force in Middlesbrough, in the North Riding of Yorkshire. The creation of the Middlesbrough Police Force dates from the 1841 Middlesbrough

Table 3.4. *Length of service in selected forces (as a percentage of intake)*

	1856	1863	1866	1876	1880
Less than one year					
Staffordshire	46	41	43	43	15
Buckinghamshire	47	34	34	33	41
		1856/60		*1866/70*	
Lancashire		42		35	
Two to five years					
Staffordshire	41	39	41	32	40
Buckinghamshire	28	36	34	34	36
		1856/60		*1866/70*	
Lancashire		30		35	
Over five years					
Staffordshire	13	20	16	24	44
Buckinghamshire	26	30	31	33	23
		1856/60		*1866/70*	
Lancashire		27		31	
Pensioners					
Staffordshire	2	13	15	10	26
Buckinghamshire	12	13	19	28	12

These figures are based on the length of service of men recruited in a specific year (in the case of Lancashire recruited over a five-year period). Pensioners are a subgroup of the total, drawn almost exclusively from those who served over five years.

Adapted from C. Steedman, *Policing the Victorian Community: The Formation of English Provincial Police Forces, 1856–80*, 1984, Table 4.3, p. 94; and W. J. Lowe, 'The Lancashire Constabulary, 1845–1870: the social and occupational function of a Victorian police force', *Criminal Justice History*, 4, 1983, Table 3, p. 55.

Improvement Act, but the early years were characterised by low pay, poor discipline and a rapid turnover of men.[53] With the appointment of a new chief officer, William Hannan, in 1853 came both an expansion in numbers and an improvement in the efficiency of the force. These developments were reinforced by the impact of the 1856 County and Borough Police Act. The force grew

Table 3.5. *Length of service of Middlesbrough recruits, 1850s to 1890s (as a percentage of the total cohort recruited in a particular decade)*

	Less than 1 year	1 to 4 years	5 to 9 years	10 to 19 years	More than 20 years	Unknown
1850s	30	25	10	2	6	28
1860s	37	21	9	3	6	24
1870s	25	34	13	5	13	11
1880s	7	41	9	14	25	4
1890s	6	27	8	38	19	2
Average	23	29	10	11	13	14

Source: Constables' Conduct Registers, CB/M/P, 29, 30 and 31, Cleveland County Archive.

from fifteen in 1861 to just under sixty a decade later and was in excess of 100 by the turn of the century.

In common with other forces, Middlesbrough saw an endless flow of men moving in and out of the police force. However, as Table 3.5 shows, an important transformation took place in the last quarter of the century. Looking at these figures, the most striking fact is the high percentage of recruits who served less than five years. At least half and probably nearer two-thirds fall into this category.[54] However, whereas a maximum of over 80 per cent of 1850s recruits fall into this category, the corresponding figure for 1890s recruits is 35 per cent. At the same time, the number of men with careers lasting more than ten years rose from less than 10 per cent to over 55 per cent. A further measure of the changes that were taking place is the fact that the mean length of completed service increased from less than three years in the period before the 1856 act to just over six years by the 1870s to reach ten years in the last two decades of the century.

Although there is merit in talking of the emergence of a long-term or career policeman in late-Victorian England, it is important to recognise the diversity of experience to be found among this relatively small group of men. Only a few men who joined in the 1850s made a long-term career of policing, that is, serving ten or more years, but those who did rose quickly through the hierarchy.

Three out of four reached the rank of inspector and one that of superintendent. As the force expanded in the 1860s there were signs that double promotion, that is beyond the rank of sergeant, was less easily achieved. Of fifteen long-term policemen, thirteen became sergeants, taking an average of five years to do so, but only seven of this number became inspectors and the rate of progress was slower, taking on average seven years and seven months. And for a minority of men there was no promotion at all; this could give rise to frustration and ill-discipline. George Dixon is a case in point. With some twenty years' experience behind him, but no promotion beyond the rank of first-class constable, his career rapidly fell apart. In June 1885 he was cautioned for neglecting to work his beat properly and reprimanded for drinking in The Bridge public house while on duty. Nine months later his pay was reduced by 2s a week for two similar offences. The downward slide continued and five months later he was absent from his beat, for which his pay was further reduced to 25s 8d a week. He was finally dismissed in 1887, having been discovered drunk in uniform.[55] It is no coincidence that a long-service class was introduced as a means of tackling this problem.

For one-third of the recruits of the 1870s, the long-service class was the final destination (Table 3.6). The numbers becoming sergeants or inspectors were significantly lower than for previous decades. What is more, promotion was taking much longer. At a time when the national average was five years, it took ten years to become a sergeant in Middlesbrough. The situation changed little in the following decade. The average length of time taken to become a sergeant rose to almost twelve years. This figure, however, obscures an important distinction. In effect there were two types of sergeant. The first was already in the long-service class before gaining promotion, a route which took on average fifteen years to complete. The second group were promoted on average after nine years, that is, before reaching the long-service class. However, of the five men who went on to become inspectors or above, three came from the first group and two from the second. For a significant number, fifteen in all, there was no promotion even to the rank of sergeant, but nine of these men did achieve the long-service class. A slight improvement for recruits of the 1880s was followed by a significant decline in the 1890s. Fewer men enlisted in these years were promoted to the ranks of sergeant and

Table 3.6. *Career patterns among long-term policemen: Middlesbrough, 1850s to 1890s (as a percentage of all long-term policemen)*

	No promotion	One promotion	Two promotions	Actual number of long-term policemen
1850s	25	75	75	4
1860s	13	87	47	15
1870s	60 (36)	40	12	25
1880s	56 (80)	44	15	34
1890s	72 (100)	28	4	50

Figures in parentheses show percentage of long-term policemen promoted to long-service class.
Source: D. Taylor, 'The standard of living of career policemen in Victorian England: the evidence of a provincial borough force', *Criminal Justice History*, 12, 1991. Adapted from Table 3, p. 120.

inspector, or above, and more men stayed as constables. However, more men received the consolation of long-service status.[56]

Change did not take place overnight, but it is clear that in the second quarter of the nineteenth century the dominant characteristics remained high turnover rates and a predominance of short-term careers. However, there were clear signs of change in the late 1870s and from the 1880s a significantly different pattern emerges. Far fewer recruits served for less than one year while far more men served for over ten years. As a consequence a more mature and more stable force came into being.

The impact of the emergence of the long-term policeman can be shown in other ways. The newly expanded force in 1857 was dominated by inexperience.[57] At the top of the Middlesbrough Police Force, Hannan had been in post for some four years (and he also had prior police experience) while Sergeant Charles Bowes had been a policeman in the town for two and a half years since leaving the York City force. The experience of the remaining eleven men was very limited. Eight had been in post for less than one year; the other three, less than two. In contrast, the Edwardian force was composed of highly experienced men. Almost two-thirds had served for more than five years and nearly a half had ten years' experience or more.

The transition to a more stable force is well illustrated in Middlesbrough by the details contained in the only surviving nominal rolls, for 1882 and 1889, summarised in Table 3.7. In 1882 the Chief Constable, the fifty-three-year-old Edward Saggerson, was a man of considerable experience.[58] With almost thirty-four years of service, twenty of which were as Chief Constable of Middlesbrough, he was supported by Superintendent Robert Thorpe, who had served just under twenty-five years, and by three inspectors (Andrew Sample, William Ashe and George Mann), all of whom were coming up to twenty years' service. A further two privately paid inspectors (John Reed and Mathew Mawer) had over twenty years' service. By 1889 Ashe had replaced Saggerson as Chief Constable – the culmination of a career that had started, rather inauspiciously, in 1866 when he was a twenty-one-year-old recruit.[59] Thorpe, now fifty-nine years old and with over thirty years' service, remained as Superintendent and Mawer, by now over fifty, was still paid for by the School Board, but there were three new inspectors (William Atkinson, Frederick Knowlson and William Peacock) with comparable experience to the men they replaced. The maturity of the force is further illustrated by the fact that in 1882 all but one of the sergeants had served for ten or more years, while in 1889 all but two had at least fifteen years' experience. Even more striking, over 80 per cent of first-class constables in 1882 had more than five years' experience, 25 per cent more than ten, and 8 per cent over fifteen. In 1889 the corresponding figures were 78 per cent, 37 per cent and 22 per cent.[60]

Middlesbrough was not a typical force, the dramatic growth of the town alone ensured that, but its pattern of development in the late nineteenth century has a more general applicability. The second generation of policing saw a consolidation and maturation of police forces across the country. Internal hierarchies were well established. There was a cadre of experienced men in senior position, many of whom, especially in the borough forces, had worked their way up through the ranks. There was a body of practical experience to hand on and, perhaps not coincidentally, the 1880s saw a number of training initiatives developed to ensure that recruits were aware of the rudiments of the job. Educational classes were also introduced for existing officers and, at the same time, the appearance of such publications as Bicknell's *Police Manual*, which was first published in 1877, was a further means of ensuring a

Table 3.7. *Rank and age structure of the Middlesbrough Borough Police Force, 1882 and 1889*

Rank	1882			1889		
	Number	% of force	Average age	Number	% of force	Average age
Chief Constable	1			1		
Superintendent	1			1		
Inspector	5			4		
All senior officers	7	11	46	6	8	47
Sergeant	10	16	39	9	13	47
PC, first class	25		36	41		37
PC, second class	7		34	5		32
PC, third class	7		30	7		27
PC, fourth class	3		25	2		26
PC, fifth class	2		22	1		21
PC, sixth class	1		67	1		40
All PCs	45	73	34	57	79	34
Total	62	100	36	72	100	37

Source: Nominal roll of the Police Force of the County Borough of Middlesbrough, September 1882 and May 1889; printed Council minutes, 25 July 1882, CB/M/C, 1/42, pp. 169–70, and 28 May 1889, CB/M/C, 1/49, pp. 234–5.

minimum standard of knowledge of their responsibilities within the law among police constables. Most importantly, policing was being seen as an occupation with its own sense of identity and worth. For a significant number of men it had ceased to be a stopgap job carried out by working-class men of little or no standing and significance in society.

Explanation of this transformation is not easy, as the voice of the police constable is rarely heard in the historical record. There are a number of inter-related factors that provide an answer. Policing was a job and, therefore, it is important to start by considering the question of wages. From a financial point of view there were, and always had been, a number of attractions to being a policeman. First and foremost, the work, and therefore the pay, was regular. Policemen did not suffer from seasonal unemployment like building workers, nor did they suffer from the longer-term cyclical fluctuations that beset iron and steel workers.

In addition, a policeman could look forward to promotion. There was a deliberate policy of recruiting from the ranks and in the borough forces, though not the county, it was possible for a man to move to the very top of the hierarchy. Not all would achieve such exulted heights and some never moved beyond the rank of constable. Nonetheless, there was a promotional ladder up which all men could expect to climb at least a few rungs. And at the end of his career a policeman could hope, and after 1890 expect, to receive a pension.

Furthermore, there were important perks to the job. In several forces, subsidised housing was available. Others provided coal. Some paid gas and water bills. There could even be assistance with the payment of local rates. And then there was the question of clothing and footwear. Policemen were provided with a uniform and were often given their old uniform for use off duty. Boot allowances were paid, though this was usually 'adjusted to pay'. And finally, for the more senior men were a small number of additional posts, such as acting as assistant Poor Law relieving officer, which could bring in a few extra pounds a year. Escorting prisoners, attending trials at quarter sessions or assizes, or even acting as a javelin man at assizes, could be a useful addition to the wages of a long-serving constable who had not moved far up the promotional ladder.[61]

There were also unofficial perks, several of which were frowned upon by the police authorities. One cannot say how common they were, but anecdotal evidence seems to suggest that most policemen were able to take advantage of such perks at some time in their career. An entrepreneurial bobby could earn a shilling or two by acting as a 'knocker-up'.[62] In many towns policemen expected to travel by tram for free and to receive complimentary tickets to the music halls, theatres, and cinemas they protected.[63] Free food and drink could come in a variety of forms. The surreptitious cup of tea and a slice of cake had become a commonplace in *Punch* and could be overlooked. Similarly, the gift of a few eggs or some vegetables to the local rural bobby was a practice that was condoned by senior officers, not least because they themselves were known to be recipients of gifts of game! However, the strategically placed pint of beer (let alone an outright request for a free pint) or other such gifts could be more problematic for the police authorities but were, nonetheless, a welcome addition to the ordinary constable.[64]

This is not to suggest that wages and pensions were un-problematic. Dissatisfaction with rates of pay and concerns with pension rights were ongoing issues, often rumbling away just below the surface of public perception, occasionally erupting into more public conflict. There were at least five petitions for improved pay submitted by the police of York between 1838 and 1853, and the watch committee, albeit reluctantly, recognised the need to improve wage levels if they were to overcome the problem of 'obtaining men of good character and ability'. In 1847, for example, the committee having sought information on wage rates in other Yorkshire towns, an increase was sanctioned.[65] In some instances there were spectacular police actions over wages. In 1853 there were major disputes in Manchester and Hull which involved mass resignations, following the refusal of the respective watch committees to respond positively to a petition for increased wages. Aided by a dispute in the local cotton trade, the Manchester policemen were able to gain an increase of 2s (10p) per week and almost total reinstatement. The lack of comparable leverage meant that the Hull men were less successful. There were problems in the Metropolitan Police, with mass protests and refusals to work in the early 1870s and again in the late 1880s.[66] But these were the tips of icebergs. A perusal of watch committee minutes reveals a continuing dissatisfaction with rates of pay, especially among the lower ranks and long-serving men. Comparisons with local trades or other forces were commonly made and adjustments made with varying degrees of goodwill. Pensions likewise led to campaigns both local and national until legislation passed in 1890 granted long-serving policemen a pension by right.

The questions remain: what, if any, were the financial benefits of becoming a policeman, and did they improve over the course of the late nineteenth century? No clear-cut answers can be given but there is evidence to suggest that there were tangible benefits for a man, especially if he was an unskilled labourer, in joining the police in the 1850s and 1860s (Table 3.8), and that policemen gained perhaps more than many working-class men during the so-called Great Depression of the late nineteenth century. The figures in Table 3.8 show clearly the monetary gains to be made by some men. The figures for Durham, however, are consistent with the known difficulties of recruiting to forces in relatively high-wage areas.

Table 3.8. *Comparative earnings, after rent, of farm labourers and police recruits, selected counties, 1860s (shillings and pence per week)*

	Farm labourer	Police recruit
Devon, 1861	6s 6d – 13s 6d	13s 11d
Durham, 1861	13s 6d – 20s	14s 7d
Buckingham, 1868	9s 0d – 14s 6d	14s 1d
		15s 1d – 16s*
Stafford, 1868	9s 6d – 14s	17s 1d – 18s 7d

* Allowing for subsidised housing.
Adapted from C. Steedman, *Policing the Victorian Community: The Formation of English Provincial Police Forces, 1856–80*, 1984, Table 5.2, pp. 11–12.

Wage rates increased steadily during the second half of the nineteenth century. The mean weekly wage in the counties in the late 1850s ranged from 16s 7d in Gloucestershire to 20s in Cheshire. By the early 1870s the figures were 19s 6½d in Devon and Dorset and 24s 9½d in Lancashire, and by the early twentieth century 23s 7½d in Dorset and 29s 5½d in Durham and Lancashire. Rates of pay varied more in the boroughs but the same upward trend is evident. Between 1857 and 1880 the median wage rate for first-class constables rose from 20s to 27s. Rates tended to be higher in the north of England, but even here there were considerable variations. In 1879 the lowest-paid received 28s in Hartlepool compared with 31s in Gateshead and Southport and 31s 6d in Durham City. Wage rates continued to grow and the median wage for a first-class constable had risen to 30s by the early twentieth century. However, despite the growing awareness of variations in pay and the use of comparability claims, considerable variations remained in pre-war English boroughs. Pay on appointment in northern England varied from 25s in Wolverhampton and 26s in Dewsbury, Preston, Walsall and Wakefield to 30s in Liverpool and St Helens. After five years' service many boroughs were paying 30s per week, though the figure for men in Liverpool and Manchester was 34s.

Given that food prices in particular were falling in the last quarter of the nineteenth century, the Victorian policeman saw his living standards rise. However, wage rate data, especially if taken in isolation, provide a crude measure of change. A more sensitive approach would look at actual earnings and relate them to the experiences of other workers. The findings for one town throw some interesting light on the changing material wellbeing of the Victorian policeman.[67]

Middlesbrough was a Victorian boom town noted for the high wages paid in the iron and steel industry. It drew men from all parts of the country. The Middlesbrough Police Force was recruited largely from unskilled workers drawn from either the rural districts of surrounding counties or the town itself. Wages were of paramount importance if men were to be attracted to and retained in the force.

The first detailed figures relate to the early 1870s. At this time there was a clear monetary benefit for a labourer joining the Police Force. In 1871 a constable on appointment received 22s per week. Agricultural labourers in the North Riding of Yorkshire received 13s 6d and those near Stockton, County Durham, received 15s 4d, while a labourer in the Middlesbrough blast furnaces could earn more, 19s a week in 1876. In other words, these men could increase their wage rates by one-third to a half by becoming a policeman. This was a powerful incentive, notwithstanding the demands of the job. After five years' service, and assuming no blemishes to the disciplinary record, a man would earn 26s as a first-class constable. This was exactly the same as a fitter, turner or patternmaker would receive in the town's engineering industries but less than boilermakers, who would receive between 30s and 31s 6d.

The boom in the local iron and steel industry put pressure on the watch committee to raise wages. By 1880 a first-class constable earned 30s and a first-class sergeant 35s a week. In local trades engineers received 31s 6d and boilermakers 29s. At the blast furnaces wages could be as high as 42s for keepers, 34s for masons and 31s for fitters, smiths, joiners and metal carriers. On the other hand, coke fillers, weighmen and keepers' helpers earned 21s a week and labourers less than £1. The increase in police wages had gone some way to preventing the haemorrhage of labour but it remained the case that the police were well paid only in relation to unskilled labourers. And this was to remain the case in subsequent years, notwithstanding the introduction of a merit class and long-service class. By the early twentieth century a fourth-class constable would earn 27s, after his six-month probationary period. Three years later he would be a first-class constable earning 30s a week. Seven years after appointment on probation came promotion

Table 3.9. *Real wages in Middlesbrough, 1871–1913, various occupations (1889 = 100)*

	1871	1876	1880	1889	1907	1913
Puddlers	121	110	100	100	138	128
Building trades	–	97	90	100	123	–
Agricultural labourers						
Stockton	69	–	85	100	105	–
North Riding	74	–	95	100	–	–
Woodworking trades	–	88	90	100	121	–
Engineering trades	69	89	82	100	113	113
Boilermakers	80	89	82	100	103	105
PC on appointment	74	85	90	100	110	110
PC, first class	73	89	90	100	100	97
PC, third class	–	–	–	–	110	110
Sergeant on appointment	74	85	90	100	110	110
Sergeant, first class	73	88	90	100	103	104
Sergeant, third class	–	–	–	–	110	116

–, data not available.
Source: D. Taylor, 'The standard of living of career policemen in Victorian England: the evidence of a provincial borough force', *Criminal Justice History*, 12, 1991, Table 6, p. 127.

to the first service class, which brought an additional shilling a week. Promotions to the second and third service classes came after further five-year intervals. In other words, a constable not gaining promotion but with a clean disciplinary record could be earning a weekly wage of 33s after seventeen years' service.[68]

Earnings in other industries put these figures into context. Engineers in the early twentieth century could expect to earn 35s 9d and boilermakers 32s 3d. In the iron and steel industry wages varied considerably. At the top, keepers earned 60s a week, metal carriers 50s and chargers and mine fillers 42s. In the intermediary category were slaggers earning 37s, keepers' helpers and enginemen 35s and coke fillers 31s 6d. Among the lowest-paid workmen were weighmen, who received 24s 6d and labourers 19s. In other words, compared with unskilled labourers, policemen were well paid but for the long-serving career policeman, comparisons with other groups of workers were less favourable.

Table 3.10. *Growth rates (% per annum) of real earnings for three career categories in the Middlesbrough Police Force, 1850s to 1890s*

	Two promotions	One promotion	No promotion
1850s/60s	2.1 to 2.6	2.1	–
1870s	2.4 to 3.6	1.4 to 2.8	1.4
1880s	3.5	1.5 to 1.7	0.6
1890s	2.5 to 3.5	1.4 to 1.8	0.3 to 0.7

Source: D. Taylor, 'The standard of living of career policemen in Victorian England: the evidence of a provincial borough force', *Criminal Justice History*, 12, 1991, Table 7, p. 127.

Relating these wage data to change in the cost of living gives the results shown in Table 3.9. These figures suggest that policing became relatively more remunerative in the period under consideration. However, in light of the earlier information on police careers, these figures should be seen as a crude indicator only. Long-term policemen fell into three categories, those achieving no, one or two promotions. An alternative approach to that adopted in Table 3.9 is to calculate real earnings figures for representative individuals in each of these categories. Table 3.10 gives the findings according to decade of recruitment. These figures should be compared with those in Table 3.11, which relate to twenty and twenty-five years' experience in three major local industries.

Table 3.11. *Growth rates (% per annum) of real earnings in three Middlesbrough industries, by length of experience, 1870s to 1890s*

	Blast furnaces		Puddling		Engineering	
	20 years	25 years	20 years	25 years	20 years	25 years
1870s	n.a.	n.a.	–1.4	0.4	1.0	1.4
1880s	0.9	1.1	0.9	1.4	0.8	1.4
1890s	0.1	0.7	0.3	1.9	0.0	0.2

Source: D. Taylor, 'The standard of living of career policemen in Victorian England: the evidence of a provincial borough force', *Criminal Justice History*, 12, 1991, Table 8, p. 128.

The figures in Tables 3.10 and 3.11 suggest that in terms of real earnings, irrespective of any perks, policing was an attractive alternative for much of the period, with the important exception of those men recruited in the 1890s who did not achieve promotion. This is not to say that pay was not an issue in the Middlesbrough force but to suggest that on balance the advantages outweighed the disadvantages. There was a degree of security about police work which contrasted with the uncertainties that surrounded an iron and steel trade faced with ever-increasing foreign competition. Even engineering, which had experienced a steady growth in real earnings in the late nineteenth century, was facing difficulties in the 1900s. Certainly there is little evidence to suggest that there was a major recruitment problem with this particular cohort. Among long-serving policemen the combined resignation and dismissal rate stayed roughly constant at 10 per cent, or just below, of the cohort.

Economic considerations are of central importance but three other factors deserve attention: first, the changing nature of the job; second, the changing standing of policing in the public eye; and third, the growth of an internal police culture and identity.

In certain respects, policing became less arduous over the course of time. Hours of work were reduced, meal breaks introduced and holiday entitlements recognised. The introduction of a guaranteed pension reduced the need to work for thirty or more years, as some of the early men had done (often to their physical detriment). In other ways conditions also improved. The provision of canteen and rest-room facilities with bagatelle and billiard tables, the opening of reading rooms with illustrated and comic papers, and the creation of police bands and sporting clubs, although serving a dual function, eased some of the worst excesses of the job.[69] The underlying hard graft remained, beats still had to be worked, the job remained physically demanding, not to mention dangerous at times, but there was some easing of conditions compared with those facing the first generation of policemen.

It is also the case that the standing of the policeman in the community improved. The police were seen to play an important role in maintaining order in the streets and combating petty crime. The decline of serious crime, although probably due more to other factors, also reflected favourably on them. Among the middle classes of late-Victorian and Edwardian England there was a widespread, if condescending, affection for the 'bobby'. There were still criticisms, usually of too little being done but also of infringements upon liberty, and the concern for 'value for money' was never far away. Nonetheless, the balance had changed. The police were praised for their actions in the pages of the local press. Brave actions at a fire or in stopping a runaway horse regularly received praise. There is also evidence of a more positive public attitude, particularly among the middle classes, reflected in a greater willingness to come to the aid of a policeman. The working classes, for the most part, were not so enthusiastic. Nonetheless, there was a shift from antagonism to acquiescence, even in some cases to affection. This is not to say that hostility and outright violence had disappeared. Even in Edwardian England, mistrust and dislike of the police could easily lead to violence in sensitive situations. However, there was a sense in which familiarity brought a tacit acceptance of the police which reduced some of the early hostility to the new police per se.

However, probably the most important factor was the development of a police culture with a positive self-image that emphasised the value of the policeman's job. These developments necessarily depended upon time. Only with time could a sense of belonging emerge. Only with time did senior officers fully appreciate the need to build up morale and how best to do so. But other factors played their part. The 1856 act, with its inspections and measures of 'efficiency', helped create a sense of pride in the team. Shared experiences at work and shared experiences off duty were further contributory factors. It is impossible to measure the impact of simply belonging to a police football or swimming team but, for example, the sight of Chief Constable William Ashe, photographed sitting at the centre of the Middlesbrough police cricket team in the 1880s, composed of men of all ranks, symbolises a unity (albeit hierarchical and paternalistic) that is rarely, if ever, discerned in the police force of the mid-nineteenth century.[70]

Other developments were important. There was a growing sense of awareness of other forces, of being part of a nationwide team. Government inspection was important here but more so was the growth of in-house journals, such as the *Police Service Advertiser* or *Police Review and Parade Gossip*, in which even ordinary constables could express their views and from which they could learn of others. In these ways there developed an *esprit de corps* that added to the sense of identity of the force.

Yet more important was the development of an identity – that of 'the loyal servant'. The image of the devoted servant was cultivated by the middle classes. The avuncular figures to be found in the pages of *Punch* did not always accord with the reality of a macho 'canteen culture' but, more importantly, some policemen developed a more positive image of themselves and their work – an image that could be articulated through contributions to in-house journals or in evidence given to select committees; an image that was reinforced in the obituaries of long-serving men.

Set apart from the communities they policed, policemen developed an ethos that stressed both loyalty to one another and service to the community. The nature of the job, particularly watching while others slept, lent itself to the development of a self-image of the faithful and trustworthy servant. From the 1870s, and possibly before, there is evidence that policemen saw their work as a craft or trade. However inappropriate to outside eyes, there was a belief that they served an apprenticeship, gaining a basic knowledge of the law and learning the practicalities of working the beat. In several forces night classes were introduced which further added to this sense of 'professionalism'.[71] Again, government inspection was an important contributory factor.

In a wider sense, policemen were expected to set an example to others in their conduct. Not every recruit matched up to these high expectations but many did internalise these values and saw themselves as part of a force for good. Theirs was to be a life governed by such virtues as obedience, sobriety and decency. Police manuals stressed the importance of personal conduct. It was not uncommon to find references, for example in police journals, to the idea of the man made good by becoming a policeman. As he journeyed through life, being rewarded for good as he moved up the hierarchy and finally received his pension, the idealised policeman became a latter-day figure from Bunyan. Moreover, as he saved himself, so he could and did save others, and in so doing he helped to uphold social order. Richard Jervis, for one, openly talked of his work in terms of a crusade. Clearly not every policeman subscribed to, let alone lived up to, such ideals. There were those who were unable to do so and those who chose not to do so. However, it would be overly cynical to deny the emergence of this important sense of self-worth.

Moreover, changes took place and were recognised by members of the public. Affectionate, if somewhat patronising, obituaries in local papers gave praise to worthy servants of the community.

Accountability and consent

The idea of the police as servants of the community was central to the thinking of nineteenth-century police reformers. From the very outset, they stressed that the police were accountable not just to the law but also to the public. The decision to retain the historic title 'constable' was important in this respect. It was widely held that the old constables had been drawn from the local communities in which they lived and were directly responsible to those they served. The continuity of the title was consciously used as a device to develop the belief that the new police were similarly accountable to the people and thereby drew their legitimacy from the people. This view persists in the orthodox histories, such as those of Critchley and Ascoli, but has been vigorously attacked by revisionist historians, such as Foster and Storch, who have hotly denied that 'the people' controlled the police and have pointed instead to the influence of the middle classes, particularly in the boroughs.[72]

Before looking more closely at this question, it is essential to outline the three different forms of policing and control that came into existence between 1829 and 1856. First, and quite distinct, was the Metropolitan Police. Like no other force in the country, they were directly responsible to the Home Office via the two commissioners of police, who were also justices of the peace. Constables were appointed and dismissed, their duties determined and their conditions of work laid down by the commissioners, though technically subject to the approval of the Home Secretary. Recruits were sworn in as constables and had the powers of a constable at common law.[73]

The 1835 Municipal Corporations Act created a different system of control for borough forces. Elected council members were required to appoint from their number a watch committee, which, along with the mayor, who was declared to be a justice of the peace, was responsible for the appointment, discipline and dismissal of police constables. No mention was made of the appointment of a chief constable though most boroughs in fact appointed a person, variously titled superintendent of police, head constable or chief constable. Local responsibility was maintained as the Home Office had no formal authority over watch committees. It was also the case that constables, as well as retaining their powers at common law, were required to obey the lawful instructions of a justice of the peace, but no one was given specific statutory responsibility for the day-to-day control of the police force. The crucial point to stress, however, is the role of the watch committee. Its right to hire or fire all constables, including chief constables, gave it considerable power, in theory.

Local responsibility, not surprisingly, was reaffirmed by the 1839 Rural Constabulary Act, but whereas borough forces now came under the responsibility of elected council members in the counties, the magistrates in quarter session had the power to establish a police force and were responsible for appointments. The Home Office had limited influence via the right to issue regulations concerning the conduct and pay of constables and the right to approve chief constables. Unlike his borough counterpart, a county chief constable, once appointed, had a far greater degree of autonomy of action. The situation in the counties was modified in 1888 when, under the Local Government Act, the establishment and management of county forces was made the responsibility of a joint standing committee of the county council, providing half the members, and of the county quarter sessions, appointing the other half. However, by this time the chief constables in the counties had established a substantial degree of independence of action.

Central control, outside the Metropolitan Police district, was very limited, particularly before 1856. The County and Borough Police Act of that year was essentially a piece of consolidating legislation but it did empower the Crown to appoint three inspectors, who were required to inspect police forces to ensure efficiency and to report to Parliament. Forces serving populations in excess of 5,000 and deemed to be efficient received an Exchequer grant amounting to one-quarter of the cost of pay and clothing. This figure was raised to a half by the Police (Expenses) Act of 1874. There was conflict between the inspectors and local authorities on more than one occasion. York received a scathing report in 1856 which aroused the wrath of members of the city council. In the following year the inspector responsible for the north of England identified further problems and the certificate of efficiency was once again refused. By now local attitudes were changing and the council saw that it could gain from the Treasury grant. In other parts of the country the combination of inspection and grants was, for the most part, successful. Most counties were deemed to be efficient from the outset. Six of the seven counties that had not qualified for a grant in the first year did so in 1857/58. The only county in which a problem persisted was Rutlandshire. The boroughs were more varied. The largest, that is, those with populations in excess of 20,000, were comparable to the counties in terms of efficiency. The problem cases were Ashton-under-Lyne, Macclesfield, Oldham and especially Stockport. Some boroughs, such as Sheffield in 1862/63, lapsed briefly into inefficiency, but for the most part there were no major long-term problems. Medium-sized boroughs were more varied but the number of inefficient forces was reduced from 50 per cent to 16 per cent by 1870. Inefficient boroughs were concentrated in the north-west and, to a lesser extent, south-west of England. In the former, insufficient numbers was a persistent problem. Inspector Woodford 'had every reason to be satisfied with the state and general appearance of this police force [in Bolton] but ... it is far from being sufficient in numbers'. In the latter there was a more general problem of inefficiency. In Dorchester, Inspector Willis found 'several old and inefficient constables, who were not clothed or organised as a regular force'. Even more problematic were the small boroughs of less than 5,000, which did not qualify for a grant and were, in effect, beyond the influence of the inspectors. The inspectors undoubtedly had a part to play in the development of borough forces in particular. Their comments on inadequate numbers and the need for amalgamations played an important part in the creation of larger forces which, in turn, created conditions more favourable to the emergence of the managerial autonomy of the chief constables.[74]

The peculiar position of the chief constable in a county force meant that there were no significant conflicts between him and the local magistrates. Indeed, the landed background of many of the early county chief constables ensured that they had a common interest with many of the magistrates.[75] In contrast, in the boroughs the situation was quite different and more fraught. Chief constables were clearly employees of the watch committee and their social origins were different. The early borough chief constables were, almost without exception, policemen who had worked their way up, often moving from a small to a larger force.

Although responsibility for the day-to-day running of the police had not been made clear, in many boroughs members of the watch committee sought to influence matters. Critchley argues that the control of the watch committee was absolute and cites in support the dismissal of the Chief Constable of Norwich for proceeding against a licensee without the express permission of the brewer-dominated watch committee. Undoubtedly there were examples of direct interference, which may or may not have been linked to the direct interests of watch committee members.[76] However, there is not sufficient evidence available to state categorically that this was typical. There is also evidence to suggest that borough chief constables were able to exercise a degree of independence based on their skill and experience in running day-to-day policing matters. In Liverpool, as early as the 1850s, the head constable had taken considerable responsibility for routine policing. The numerous organisational directives that he issued went unchallenged by members of the watch committee. Alternatively, where members of the watch committee demanded police action, usually because of disorderly street behaviour, profaning of the Sabbath and a variety of moral offences such as prostitution and gambling, it became increasingly the practice to refer matters to the head constable for his attention.[77] Effectively, the role of the chief constable grew out of the difficulties faced by members of a watch committee with limited time and expertise in policing matters. This became increasingly apparent as the size of borough forces grew, not least because of enforced amalgamations, in the late nineteenth century.[78] In a different, and not wholly intended, way the autonomy of the chief constable was increased by certain pieces of legislation, such as the 1861 Explosives Act or the 1875 Adulterated Foods Act, which created a direct line between the government and local police chiefs.[79]

There were two major incidents of conflict between a chief constable and his watch committee that deserve further attention. The first of these took place in Birmingham in 1880. The Chief Constable decided on his own initiative to change existing practice by proceeding against all drunks, irrespective of whether they were disorderly or not. In the following year, acting as 'the guardian of public morality and order', he attempted (without success) to prosecute a music-hall manager for staging improper performances. The watch committee demanded an explanation of his actions and resolved that any further changes in policy should be first reported to the watch committee. The Chief Constable refused to accept this unless ordered to do so by the Home Office or the magistrates. The Home Secretary refused to intervene in the matter and the magistrates refused to interfere in arrangements between the watch committee and the Chief Constable. Lacking support, the Chief Constable gave way but the fundamental issue of responsibility remained unresolved.

Even more spectacular was the dispute in Liverpool that broke out following an order by the Head Constable in 1890 to 'proceed against all brothels at present known to the police without any delay'. The matter has been interpreted in a variety of ways. Generally, the emphasis has been on the subservience of the Head Constable to the watch committee. The reality is more complex. The Head Constable, Nott-Bower, actually advised against wholesale prosecution. He defended his discretionary approach partly in terms of his common-law powers but also partly in terms of his (and others') experience in dealing with such matters. Nott-Bower's judgement was over-ruled and he accepted the decision of the watch committee to start action. The policy was a failure and Nott-Bower defended himself on the grounds that he was simply acting on the decision of the watch committee. However, it would be wrong to conclude from this that Nott-Bower was a subservient figure. On the contrary, by emphasising his experience, as well as his powers as a constable under common law, Nott-Bower was able to make a case for his managerial independence in the exercise of the police function.

The Liverpool case raises a number of important points. First, it casts doubt on the simplistic view of watch committee influence. Watch committees were not homogeneous bodies and there was rarely a long-term dominant influence. The fluctuating fortunes of local politics necessarily affected policing in varied ways. Second, it throws into question the whole issue of accountability via the democratic process. If, as seems to be the case, chief constables like Nott-Bower were establishing the principle and practice of managerial autonomy this weakened the claim of 'democratic responsibility' that was made for the police. This in turn had important implications for the question of policing by consent.

Finally, we need to turn briefly to the question of popular support for the police. The need for the police to win at least the tacit support of a majority of the population in order to function in the long term is obvious. The fact that there was popular opposition is equally well known (and will be discussed more fully in the next chapter) but the question remains: to what extent had the police achieved this degree of support by the early twentieth century? Before attempting to answer this question it is necessary to look more closely at the concept of consent with regard to policing. Given the nature of nineteenth-century society, the priorities embedded in the law and the nature of practical policing, it is hardly surprising to discover that police work was inherently conflict ridden. Albeit for very different reasons, both orthodox and revisionist historians tend to adopt an oversimplified and unrealistic notion of consent.[80] It is unrealistic to expect to find near-universal support and affection for the police, but the persistence of anti-police sentiments and actions do not in themselves necessarily invalidate the claim to have achieved policing by consent. The crucial distinction is between a dislike of (and even a violent response to) a specific police action and a general rejection of the legitimacy of the police per se.

There is clear evidence of this fundamental rejection of policing in certain districts following the introduction of the new police. The police, as a body, were literally driven out of some towns. However, the extension of police forces to the counties and boroughs of England and their continuing existence is prima facie evidence of success in gaining the necessary degree of consent.

Notes

1   The distinction between 'rough' and 'respectable' is by no means clear cut. The terms were often used uncritically by Victorian commentators to distinguish between the middle and working classes and between the 'deserving' and 'undeserving' elements of the latter. Such usage, which persists in some of the historical literature, is unhelpful as it obscures important variations not only within classes but also in the behaviour of small social groups and even individuals.

2 J. P. Martin and G. Wilson, *The Police: A Study in Manpower. The Evolution of the Service in England and Wales, 1829–1965*, London, Heinemann, 1969, p. 32.

3 P. T. Smith, *Policing Victorian London*, Connecticut, Greenwood Press, 1985, p. 42.

4 S. Petrow, *Policing Morals: The Metropolitan Police and the Home Office, 1870–1914*, Oxford, Oxford University Press, 1994, p. 37.

5 Report of the Select Committee on the Police of the Metropolis, *Parliamentary Papers*, 1834, xvi, pp. 418–19.

6 The position worsened in the following decade, when 37 per cent of recruits served less than one year, 58 per cent less than five years with a further 24 per cent 'unknown', who almost certainly served only a short time. D. Taylor, 'The standard of living of career policemen in Victorian England: the evidence of a provincial borough force', *Criminal Justice History*, 12, 1991, Table 1, p. 108.

7 C. Steedman, *Policing the Victorian Community: The Formation of English Provincial Police Forces, 1856–80*, London, Routledge, Kegan and Paul, 1984, p. 94.

8 W. J. Lowe, 'The Lancashire Constabulary, 1845–1870: the social and occupational function of a Victorian police force', *Criminal Justice History*, 4, 1983, Table 3, p. 55.

9 Martin and Wilson, *The Police*, p. 13.

10 *Ibid*.

11 Steedman, *Policing*, p. 93. There were some interesting variations. The turnover in West Sussex in 1880 was as high as that for Cheshire and the North Riding of Yorkshire and higher than that of any other northern county. Similarly, Hampshire, with a turnover of 15 per cent, had a worse record in this respect than Durham, Lancashire and the West Riding of Yorkshire. Northumberland and Nottingham, by contrast, experienced turnovers of only 8 and 7 per cent respectively – figures exceeded by six southern counties in 1880.

12 Cited in Steedman, *Policing*, pp. 92–3.

13 *Ibid*., Table 4.5, pp. 98–101.

14 *Ibid*., pp. 86–7.

15 Lowe, 'Lancashire Constabulary', pp. 47–8.

16 Steedman, *Policing*, p. 81; Lowe, 'Lancashire Constabulary', p. 46.

17 H. Shpayer-Makov, 'A portrait of a novice constable in the London Metropolitan Police, c. 1900', *Criminal Justice History*, 12, 1991, p. 139.

18 A large majority of constables were married and this was seen as a stabilising influence. However, in the early days of drilling the unmarried man was felt to be more malleable.

19 D. Philips, *Crime and Authority in Victorian England*, London, Croom Helm, 1977, p. 74.

20 Lowe, 'Lancashire Constabulary', p. 45.

21 Shpayer-Makov, 'Portrait', p. 139.

22 Report of the Select Committee on Police Superannuation Funds, *Parliamentary Papers*, 1875, xiii, Q 3041 and 3043.

23 *Ibid.*, Q 1115.

24 *Ibid.*, Q 1309. He also noted that because of higher rates of pay, he lost men to the Metropolitan Police and certain northern borough forces. See Q 1321.

25 Steedman, *Policing*, p. 85.

26 Select Committee on Police Superannuation, Q 3234.

27 *Ibid.*, Q 1803.

28 Steedman, *Policing*, p. 85.

29 *Ibid.*, p. 71.

30 Lowe, 'Lancashire Constabulary', p. 51; A. Jessop, *Arcady: for Better, for Worse*, London, Fisher Unwin, 1887, p. 117.

31 A. A. Clarke, *The Policemen of Hull*, Beverley, Hutton Press, 1992, p. 62.

32 C. T. Clarkson and J. H. Richardson, *Police!*, London, Leadenhall Press, 1888, p. 83.

33 B. D. Butcher, *'A Movable Rambling Force': An Official History of Policing in Norfolk*, Norwich, Norfolk Constabulary, 1989, p. 66; C. Emsley, *The English Police: A Political and Social History*, Hemel Hempstead, Harvester Wheatsheaf, 1991, p. 191.

34 Steedman, *Policing*, p. 122.

35 A. F. Richter, *Bedfordshire Police, 1840–1990*, Kempston, Hooley, 1990, p. 19; B. Howell, *The Police in Late-Victorian Bristol*, Bristol, Bristol Historical Association pamphlet, 1986, p. 5; Butcher, *Movable, Rambling Force*, p. 11; R. Swift, *Police Reform in Early Victorian York, 1835–1856*, York, University of York, Borthwick Papers, no. 73, 1988, pp. 15 and 56. In 1869 Ipswich policemen required the permission of the mayor before leaving the town. L. C. Jacobs, *Constables of Suffolk*, Ipswich, Suffolk Constabulary, 1992, p. 22.

36 Clarke, *Hull*, p. 38.

37 N. Pringle and J. Treversh, *150 Years Policing in Watford District and Hertfordshire County*, Luton, Radley Shaw, 1991, p. 47. A similar requirement was made of men in the East Riding and Shropshire constabularies. The latter were required to attend in full-dress uniform. A. A. Clarke, *Country Coppers: The Story of the East Riding Police*, Hornsea, Arton Books, 1993; and D. J. Elliot, *Policing Shropshire, 1836–1967*, Studley, Brewin Books, 1984. The men of the Bedfordshire police and the Luton borough force were each exhorted to attend church at least once every Sunday, though it is not clear that any exceeded the minimum. Richter, *Bedfordshire Police*; and T. J. Madigan, *The Men Who Wore Straw Hats: Policing Luton, 1840–1974*, Dunstable, Book Castle, 1993.

38 Standing order 14. 'Hair and beards', 1 January 1898, cited in Pringle and Treversh, *Watford District*, p. 7.

39 Bob Dobson, *Policing in Lancashire, 1839–1989*, Staining, Landy, 1989, p. 87.

40 That said, at least one Middlesbrough policeman was dismissed because his wife was running a shop. Pringle and Treversh, *Watford District*, p. 49; anonymous, *150 Years of Service: Essex Police, 1840–1990*, Rayleigh, Hockley, 1990, no pagination.

41 F. Thompson, *Lark Rise to Candleford*, London, Penguin, 1973, p. 484; R. Jervis, *Chronicles of a Victorian Detective*, first published 1907, reprinted Runcorn, P. and D. Riley, 1995, p. 84.

42 Clarke, *Country Coppers*, p. 47; M. Hann, *Policing Victorian Dorset*, Wincanton, Dorset Publishing, 1989, p. 4. Transfers were also used for disciplinary purposes.

43 Clarke, *Hull*, p. 24; Lowe, 'Lancashire Constabulary', p. 24; H. Shpayer-Makov, 'The making of a police labour force', *Criminal Justice History*, 24, 1990, p. 109.

44 Select Committee on the Police of the Metropolis, QQ 107–8; Hann, *Dorset*, pp. 14, 37–8.

45 Clarke, *Hull*, p. 51; D. Taylor, *999 And All That*, Oldham, Oldham Corporation, 1968, p. 63.

46 The Middlesbrough examples are taken from the Constables' Conduct Register in Cleveland County Archive, CB/M/P, 29–31, while the Worcestershire example is cited in Emsley, *English Police*, pp. 201–2. The Oldham and West Sussex examples are respectively from Taylor, *999*, p. 54, and Jacobs, *Suffolk*, pp. 20, 42.

47 Anonymous, *150 Years of Service*.

48 Jacobs, *Suffolk*, p. 36; Elliot, *Shropshire*, pp. 20–1.

49 Clarke, *Country Coppers*, pp. 22–4.

50 See also the tables produced by William Farr for the Select Committee on Police Superannuation Funds, especially Table xlvii.

51 Shpayer-Makov, 'Making of a police labour force', pp. 109–10.

52 For example, Richard Jervis, whose father had been a Lancashire police officer, joined at the early age of eighteen years in 1850. Jervis, *Chronicles*.

53 D. Taylor, 'Crime and policing in early Victorian Middlesbrough, 1835–55', *Journal of Regional and Local Studies*, 11, 1991.

54 The records for the early years are patchy, hence the high number recorded as 'unknown'. It is highly probable that these men served for only a very short time as there is no other evidence of long service in the force.

55 A similar case is that of Robert Gatenby, which illustrates the point well. Appointed a third-class constable in 1866, he had risen to the first class and been awarded a merit badge in 1874. Thereafter his career hit difficulties. He lost his merit badge for being drunk on duty at the parliamentary election of February 1874. He made good the financial loss but was never promoted. Ten years later, still on the same grade, matters came to a head. In March 1884 he was reduced to the third class and lost forty-four days' pay for being drunk on duty. Four months later he was ordered to resign, having assaulted a member of the public.

56 For further details of the careers of individual long-term policemen see Taylor, 'Standard of living'.

57 The following details are taken from the Constables' Conduct Register, CB/M/C, 2/100, 10 March 1857, Cleveland County Archive.

58 Saggerson had served almost four years in the Lancashire constabulary and ten years in Oldham. During this period he rose to the rank of inspector and was involved in a series of complaints that led to the dismissal of the Head Constable of Oldham. Select Committee on Police Superannuation Funds, Q 3232; and Taylor, *999*, p. 126.

59 Ashe's rise to fame, which included a dramatic journey to Melbourne, Australia, in pursuit of an absconding local official, is described in D. Taylor, 'The antipodean arrest: or how to be a successful policeman in nineteenth-century Middlesbrough', *Bulletin of the Cleveland and Teesside Local History Society*, 58, 1990.

60 Cleveland County Archive, printed Council minutes, CB/M/C, 1/43 (1882/83), 19 September 1882 and CB/M/C, 1/49 (1888/89), 28 May 1889.

61 Steedman, *Policing*, p. 113.

62 Thomas Cavanagh, describing policing in mid-nineteenth-century London, noted that 'there was a good deal of money to be made' by calling up men who needed to be awoken at 4 a.m. to get to work in the local markets and were prepared to pay sixpence (2½p) a week for the service. T. Cavanagh, *Scotland Yard Past and Present: Experiences of Thirty Seven Years*, London, Chatto & Windus, 1893, pp. 22–3.

63 The Metropolitan Police authorities did not take kindly to the former practice and there was a concerted effort in the 1880s to stamp it out. Emsley, *English Police*, p. 223. Other services were also expected free and there were a number of incidents involving police and prostitutes that created difficulties.

64 Such gifts could be a sign of acceptance by members of the public and provide a valuable means of improving police–community relations but there was a fine line dividing this from bribery.

65 Swift, *Police Reform*, pp. 17–18.

66 Steedman, *Policing*, pp. 133–4; Emsley, *English Police*, pp. 92–3.

67 For full details see Taylor, 'Standard of living'.

68 A similar system applied to sergeants. Twelve years after appointment as a full sergeant a man would reach the second service class, at which point he would be earning 38s 6d per week.

69 The provision of rest-rooms, complete with newspapers, was intended as much to keep off-duty policemen away from temptation, while police bands and sporting clubs were an important means of building ties with the local community. Several forces were also provided with Bibles by senior officers.

70 Shpayer-Makov, 'Making of a police labour force', p. 114; Steedman, *Policing*, chapter 8; D. Taylor, *'A Well-Chosen, Effective Body of Men': The Middlesbrough Police Force, 1841–1914*, Teesside Papers in North Eastern History, no. 6, Middlesbrough, University of Teesside, 1995.

71 Strictly speaking policing cannot be seen as a profession but there was an important sense in which policemen grew to believe that they had learned knowledge and skill that set them apart from the population at large.

72 T. A. Critchley, *A History of Police in England and Wales*, London, Constable, 1979; D. Ascoli, *The Queen's Peace: The Origins and Development of the Metropolitan Police 1829–1979*, London, Hamish Hamilton, 1979; R. D. Storch, 'The plague of blue locusts: police reform and popular resistance in northern England, 1840–1857', *International Review of Social History*, 20, 1975, and 'The policeman as domestic missionary', *Journal of Social History*, 9, 1976; J. Foster, *Class Struggle and the Industrial Revolution*, London, Methuen, 1977.

73 T. Jefferson and R. Grimshaw, *Controlling the Constable: Police Accountability in England and Wales*, London, Muller, 1984, p. 28.

74 J. Hart, 'The County and Borough Police Act, 1856', *Public Administration*, 34, 1954, details improvements in buildings, beneficial changes in personnel and other positive effects achieved by the inspectors. See also H. Parris, 'The Home Office and the provincial police in England and Wales, 1856–1870', *Public Law*, 20, 1961, especially pp. 242, 244–5; Martin and Wilson, *The Police*; and M. Brogden, *The Police: Autonomy and Consent*, London, Academic Press, 1982, p. 99.

75 Many had an army background as well. The post of chief constable in a county force became an acceptable occupation for the younger sons of landed gentry, especially after the Crimean War, when promotion opportunities in the army dried up. D. Walls, 'The selection of chief constables in England and Wales, 1835–1985', unpublished MPhil thesis, University of York, 1989, p. 226. The 1888 Local Government Act did not have much effect on the social background of the second generation of county chief constables. The appointment of such people, while running contrary to the hopes of Peel, was in keeping with the rural model of society that many police reformers held.

76 Critchley, *History of the Police*, p. 143; Parris, 'Home Office', cites Cambridge, Carlisle and Liverpool as boroughs in which the brewing interest made itself felt on police practice. The role of the brewing interest in Liverpool is also noted by J. Hart, 'Reform of the borough police, 1835–1856', *English Historical Review*, 70, 1955; and Brogden, *The Police*.

77 Brogden, *The Police*, pp. 64–5.

78 Walls, 'Selection', p. 224.

79 Emsley, *English Police*, p. 88.

80 R. Reiner, *The Politics of the Police*, 2nd edn, Hemel Hempstead, Harvester Wheatsheaf, 1992, p. 59.

4

The impact of the new police: actions and reactions

In many a back street and slum he [the policeman] not only stands for law and order; he is the true handy-man of the streets, the best friend of a mass of people who have no other counsellor or protector. (*The Times*, 24 December 1908, p. 7)

Introduction

The second quarter of the nineteenth century witnessed the creation of the new police and the next fifty years saw their consolidation, but the actions of the new police and the popular responses to them were complex, controversial and often contradictory. Contemporaries, as much as later historians, were divided in their assessments. If we are to evaluate these different points of view, it is essential to examine in detail the wide range of police activities and how they impinged upon society in general and the working classes in particular.

Constabulary duties

It is essential not to adopt a one-dimensional view of the new police. They were a multi-functional body. Their roles and responsibilities ranged considerably and increased as time passed. It is important to grasp the varied nature of their work as it had a profound effect on the new policed society that was brought into being.

The General Instructions issued to all Metropolitan policemen when they started duty in 1829 provides a useful insight into the intentions of the founding fathers, Rowan and Mayne. In an oft-quoted sentence it was made clear that 'the principal object to be attained is the Prevention of Crime [and] to this great end every effort of the Police is to be directed'.[1] This unequivocal emphasis on crime prevention has figured prominently in Whig histories of the police. However, it is often overlooked that crime prevention was seen as a means to an end. From it would follow 'the security of the person and property, the preservation of the public tranquillity, and all the other objects of a Police Establishment'.[2] Furthermore, and this was to have important implications for policing in practice, it was recognised at the outset that the General Instructions were not rigid rules to be applied unquestioningly but that 'something must necessarily be left to the discretion and intelligence of the individual'.[3] Defining the role of the policeman was problematic. Discretion had to be used in determining what necessitated intervention. It was easy to say that a threat to public order should be dealt with firmly. But what constituted a threat to public tranquillity? Was it a mob bent on pillage, an unlicensed fair, a penny-gaff, a meeting of political radicals, a strike, a church band, or an animated group of young men outside a public house? There were endless possibilities, all of which carried considerable scope for conflict. One thing, however, is abundantly clear. The arrival of the policeman on the streets and in the lanes of England meant that the people, and particularly the working classes, were being subjected to an unprecedented degree of scrutiny and control over a wide range of activities, many of which were seen to be legitimised by long-established custom. As Storch has forcefully argued, the police were expected 'to maintain a constant, unceasing pressure of surveillance upon all facets of life in working-class communities,' and as such represented a 'significant increase' in theory, if not always in practice, of 'the moral and political authority of the state'.[4] War was waged not simply on crime but also on the custom and cultures of the people.

The Metropolitan Police guidance was taken up, often word for word, by other forces in England. Nor was it unusual for constables to be given extensive advice on their role and responsibilities. Birmingham is a case in point.[5] Great emphasis was placed on defending the public against thefts, assaults and breaches of the peace such as riots and affrays but it was also clear that police duties went beyond this. There was a welfare role that encompassed 'insane persons and children ... wandering in the streets,' but also a clear concern with maintaining standards of decency. Constables were to arrest people exhibiting obscene prints, not to mention those who were exhibiting themselves 'with intent to insult any female'. Street prostitutes, beggars, gamblers and those simply wandering with no visible means of sustenance or not giving a good account of themselves were liable to arrest. Such concerns were not confined to the cities. In King's Lynn the police superintendent was given clear instructions in 1836 'to patrol the ground for the purpose of suppressing vagrancy and to inspect the Public Houses and Beer Houses'.[6]

The range of police activities was increased as changes in legislation brought new responsibilities. The state extended its powers in an attempt to reform the morals of the people. Drinking, gambling and prostitution came under increasing pressure. Indeed, by the early twentieth century the police responsibilities had extended to include, among others, offences under the elementary education acts, offences relating to adulterated food, cruelty to animals, cruelty to children, and the licensing of dogs and explosives. They checked and acted against people acting as hawkers, pedlars or porters without certificates, old-metal dealers, and child street traders. They had to deal with a range of quasi-criminal matters, such as various forms of maintenance. The police dealt with matters relating to bastardy orders, maintenance orders under the 1885 Summary Jurisdiction (Married Women) Act, and orders for payment of maintenance in industrial and reformatory schools. Other legislation meant that they were involved in such matters as orders granted to the husbands of habitual drunkards, orders under the 1875 Employers' and Workmen's Act or orders to pay over accounts under the 1896 Friendly Societies Act, and so on.[7]

The significance of this legislative change should not be underestimated. As well as extending police responsibilities, it also extended police power. The 1862 Night Poaching Act, for example, gave provincial police wide powers to stop and search on suspicion. Even more so, the 1879 Summary Jurisdiction Act outlined 'a nation-wide and systematised police procedure in the disciplining of social life'.[8] The serving of warrants for distress, the whipping of juveniles and general involvement in a whole gamut of activities, from watching and apprehension through to trial and punishment, fundamentally changed the relationship between police and public. It also changed the public's perception of the police for the worse. However, to some extent, this was mitigated by the creation of 'outcast' groups, upon whom police attention could be focused without alienating the bulk of the population. Legislation such as the 1869 Habitual Criminal Act and the 1871 Prevention of Crime Act enabled the police to do just this. In so doing a myth was created of a uniquely criminal and threatening group against whom the police must act. By focusing on such groups, habitual criminals, habitual drunkards but also the Irish and aliens, the police could appeal to the beliefs and prejudices of a growing number of respectable working men and women.[9]

Local bye-laws were a further element in the complex puzzle facing the constable on the beat. There were various rules and regulations relating to conduct in the street or in public parks. Furious driving of beasts, cruelty to animals, the singing of obscene songs, the flying of kites, the bowling of hoops, the playing of football, obstructing the pavement, even shaking rugs and carpets in the streets before 8 a.m., let alone throwing orange peel on the flagstones, were but a few of the offences against local bye-laws.[10] Even a cursory examination of annual police returns reveals that such offences were a major element in police work, far outweighing in number the more serious criminal offences which caught the local and national headlines.[11] What is more, such concern with what Foucault has termed the 'micro-technics' of power had a significance that went far beyond the apparent triviality of the incidents concerned.

Nor was the situation fundamentally different in rural areas. Surviving beat books, for example, reveal the mundane and petty nature of much police work. PC Richard Hann spent five years in Sixpenny Handley, Dorset, during which time he arrested people for killing hares without a licence, allowing horses to stray, keeping dogs without a licence, and so forth. New responsibilities came in the form of legislation passed to deal with the problem of contagious diseases in animals![12]

The nature of policing was also conditioned by such variables as the attitudes of the local watch committee or of the local chief constables. Nowhere can this be seen more clearly than in the handling of drunks. Fluctuations in the number of arrests for drunken and disorderly behaviour are a better guide to the beliefs of members of watch committees and/or chief constables than to real changes in such behaviour. The rise in the number of arrests for drunkenness in Birmingham in 1880 was the result of zealous action by the Chief Constable, who decided to prosecute all drunks, irrespective of whether they were or were not disorderly. In Liverpool in 1878 there was a major campaign against public houses instigated by a watch committee under pressure from the local vigilance committee and in 1890 members of the watch committee pressed for concerted action against prostitution, as mentioned in the previous chapter, which led to a major conflict with the Chief Constable.[13] In York the policing priorities set by the watch committee and magistrates centred on 'the conditions of the streets'. As well as taking a firm line with drunk and disorderly behaviour, the police were instructed to act firmly against street gambling and the breaking of the Sabbath by shopkeepers.[14] Similarly, chief constables could take the initiative. Superintendent Heaton, responsible for the 'Huddersfield Crusade', sought to improve the morals of one part of the West Riding in no uncertain terms, though, it has to be added, with limited success. Attempts were made to restrict drinking by a sustained attack on public ale and beer-houses. Cruel sports such as cockfighting and dogfighting, prize fighting and gambling also came under attack. Guy Fawkes celebrations in the town were halted in the early 1850s while, bizarrely and unsuccessfully, three men were prosecuted for watching cricket on Sunday when ordered by the police to attend church.[15]

Many chief constables were concerned with 'immorality' in its many and inter-related forms and many believed, like the Head Constable of Stockport, that the police force could be made 'the instrument not only in the promotion of public health and the prevention of crime, but also in promoting the general good of society'.[16] But few acted with the zealous manner shown in Huddersfield and Birmingham. To the contrary, many were highly sceptical of the impact they could have. Operational realities brought a different perspective on events. However, this could lead to conflict with watch committees and local pressure groups. In Middlesbrough there was a vociferous temperance lobby that did not take kindly to police tactics. Taking incapable drunks home in a wheelbarrow was not seen to be an appropriate use of police time.[17] The most spectacular conflict, however, took place in Liverpool in the late nineteenth century, though tensions had existed from the 1860s onwards. The watch committee made it clear that they viewed the proliferation of alehouses to be the cause of the vice problem in the city. However, the Head Constable, Major J. J. Greig, had doubts about the legal powers available to him and, more importantly, felt that the scale of the problem of the public houses (and associated activities) was too great for his force to cope with. Matters finally came to a head following the order to proceed against brothels mentioned above. The Head Constable, Nott-Bower, strongly advised against wholesale prosecution but his advice was over-ridden. This, and the Birmingham case, raised important questions about responsibility and accountability, as discussed in the previous chapter, but suffice it to say at this point that the thrust of policing in a particular place and time could be fundamentally altered by the determination of people with a specific view of police priorities.

Finally, it is essential to recognise the importance of the individual constable and the discretion that he exercised. It is a commonplace to observe that intention does not guarantee outcome. Legislative developments, instructions from the chairman of the watch committee and even general orders from a chief constable were not automatically translated into practice on the street. Day-to-day policing was a dark, often unrecorded, area about which one can do little more than speculate. However, it is clear from the continued complaints to and by local watch committees and the reiteration of orders by chief constables that theory and practice did not always coincide. Why this should be so is not easy to demonstrate. Incompetence and laziness played a part, as did over-zealousness, but so too did an unwillingness to enforce laws either out of sympathy for the proscribed activity – street gambling is an obvious example – or out of a sense of the danger or the futility of action. More importantly, police actions, which might vary in detail from one locality to another, were shaped by the limited resources available. This meant not only that issues had to be prioritised but that decisions were often made intuitively. In practice this would mean that certain districts, Jennings' Buildings off Kensington High Street, London, for example, or certain groups such as poor Irish, casual or migrant workers or juveniles were singled out for attention because they fitted the contemporary stereotype of the criminal.[18]

The way in which the constable conducted himself was also of paramount importance. Complaints about officiousness, brutality and arbitrariness can be found in most parts of the country, at one time or another. Not all were well founded but others were. The fact that men in one force had to be instructed 'not to use sticks to beat mobs with' nor to use shortened or loaded staves (with nails or lead added), life preservers or other weapons is indicative of the problems that could occur.[19] The creation of a well disciplined force was a difficult and never entirely successful operation. However, it is also important to recognise the very real practical constraints under which the police worked. It was not simply the case that they could not keep all working-class districts and activities under constant surveillance, though this was undoubtedly so, but also that they needed to win the tacit support of a majority of the population if they were to conduct their day-to-day business. In a very real sense, policing by consent and the use of minimal force were practical necessities. This fact was recognised by the first Metropolitan Police Commissioners, Rowan and Mayne, and elevated into a principle.

That said, many senior officers genuinely believed in policing by consent and actively sought to improve police–public relations. The careful consideration given by the first commissioners to complaints made against constables of the Metropolitan Police is but one well known example. Elsewhere chief constables sought to provide guidance that would improve the conduct of their constables and thus reduce public suspicion or hostility. Constables were instructed to treat members of the public with due care, but one suspects that it was the concern with middle-class hostility that lay behind instructions to proceed with caution when faced with ladies window shopping. Other steps were taken to foster good relations. The running of charitable organisations, boot funds, soup kitchens and the like, or the organising of sporting activities such as swimming galas or athletics meetings, were all part of the process.

In sum, therefore, a policeman was expected to combine a variety of roles: crime fighter, peace preserver, welfare agent and moral missionary. Moreover, the emphasis that should have been given to these roles – let alone the emphasis that was actually given to them – could vary considerably from time to time and place to place. In these circumstances it is not unreasonable to expect that popular responses would be complex and even contradictory. However, before looking at this question we must briefly consider the impact of the police on the incidence of crime.

Given the importance attached to crime prevention by the founding fathers of the new police, the crime statistics, which were published in ever-more refined form during the nineteenth century, were seen as vital evidence in the contemporary debate on police effectiveness. The official statistics, however, have to be handled with caution and cannot be taken at face value as a measure of the true incidence of crime.[20] There are a number of factors, such as an increase in the number of policemen, improvements in policing, changes in punishment and changing costs of and attitudes towards prosecution through the courts, which will artificially inflate the crime rate.

This said, it is probably the case that there was a long-term downturn in the rate of serious crime for England and Wales which probably dated from the late 1850s, and certainly from the early 1860s, and continued until the end of the century. Although there was a slight upturn in the early twentieth century, there was no return to the levels of the mid-nineteenth century.[21] There were, of course, regional variations. In London the decline began somewhat earlier whereas, in contrast, in areas such as Lancashire, the Black Country and South Wales rates of serious crime may well have increased until the 1860s before assuming a long-term downward trend.[22] Nonetheless, the general pattern of improvement holds good.

To what extent the new police were responsible for this change is problematic. Gatrell argues 'unapologetically' for the positive role of the police and the courts.[23] Pointing to ever-improving rates for arrests, prosecutions and convictions, he stresses the strengthening of the coercive power of the state as well as the vulnerability of the mid-nineteenth-century criminals to the improvements in policing. The police, in town and country, were having a deterrent effect as a result of their increased surveillance. Local research lends support to this interpretation. In Horncastle the new police, introduced in the early 1830s, appear to have been successful in reducing the number of disturbances in the town associated with public houses and brothels. Indeed, by the 1850s there had been a reduction in the number of local brothels from twenty to five.[24] The new police in

Birmingham appear to have made a discernible impact on crime in a short period of time, which facilitated their acceptance by members of the public.[25] The *Liverpool Mercury* recorded the favourable response of the inhabitants of Toxteth Park to the new police, who protected 'the public from the insolence and brutality' of the 'hordes of beggars and other disorderly characters' who had disturbed the area unchecked by the old police. Likewise in York the new police were successful in their dealing with petty crimes, though less so with serious offences. Finally, a similar picture emerges from the newly policed villages of southern England.[26]

However, certain qualifications have to be made. It does not appear to be the case that the new police had a significant role to play in the decrease of burglary, housebreaking and violent crimes. Moreover, even though they appear to have had a significant impact on larcenies there were other factors at work. It is highly probable that a general improvement in working-class living standards combined with a gradual spread of 'respectability' throughout society resulted in a society in which necessitous theft was less prominent. Similarly, a probable reduction in the levels of alcohol consumption, changing attitudes towards interpersonal violence, and a redefinition of masculinity all played their part in the diminution of violence.[27] Nonetheless, it remains the case that to many contemporaries the police appeared to be winning the battle against crime and immorality in late-nineteenth-century England.

As the rate of serious crime was decreasing, the likelihood of arrest was increasing as the new police subjected working-class society in particular to greater scrutiny and as they were charged with responsibility for regulating ever-wider areas of social and economic life. The advent of the new police revealed a large volume of hitherto unrecorded crime, predominantly of a petty nature, and this was to increase in the latter part of the nineteenth century. In a real sense, changes in the law and changes in policing created the problem of petty criminality, especially among young, working-class juveniles.

Popular responses: London

The proposal to create a police force in London had been unpopular with many sections of the population of London and its appearance aroused considerable and widespread hostility. The earliest police histories give a heroic description, with strong religious overtones, of the advent of the new police. In a chapter headed 'Early suffering and martyrdom', Charles Reith gave an account that consciously or otherwise parallels the story of the early Christians. Faced with initial opposition on all sides, physically and verbally assaulted, 'their triumph over their incredible sufferings' is part of 'the wonder of the miracle of what the New Police achieved,' as they showed that 'nationally-characteristic instinct for doing what had to be done and doing it fearlessly and unflinchingly'. This, it is argued, was clearly the case during the disturbances at Cold Bath Fields in 1833, when the unfortunate PC Culley was killed. Despite an initial verdict of 'justifiable homicide' in the coroner's court, the official enquiry revealed the hostility directed at the police and vindicated their actions. As a consequence the public in London, having experienced a conversion as dramatic as Paul's on the road to Damascus, saw the new police as the bringers of 'peace and security ... in place of turmoil and lawlessness'. Thus, according to Reith, 'the efficient action and complete success of the police at Cold Bath Fields in 1833 mark the beginning of a new and more friendly relationship between them [the London public] and the police'.[28]

Later historians have given a more qualified interpretation. Middle-class attitudes may well have been changing earlier, that is, during the Reform disturbances preceding the great 1832 Reform Act. This did not mean the end of criticisms, especially those directed at the expense of policing, but it is significant that criticisms were increasingly to be found couched in terms of too little rather than too much police action. However, while accepting that middle-class Londoners, as the major and most direct beneficiaries, 'enthusiastically supported' the new police, Wilbur Miller concedes that working-class acceptance of the police was 'fragile and ambivalent'.[29] Contrary to earlier beliefs that opposition was confined solely to the rough and criminal elements of working-class society, the respectable working classes were often suspicious of, if not hostile to, the neighbourhood bobby. Attitudes fluctuated over time. Initial hostility in the 1830s and 1840s was replaced by a growing level of tolerance, punctuated, it is true, by a number of spectacular disturbances in the third quarter of the century. However, tensions and conflicts appear to have increased in the 1880s and 1890s.

To understand popular attitudes it is necessary to look more closely at the development of various aspects of policing in London. Fears that the new police posed a threat to constitutional liberty were expressed by members of the radical vestries in districts such as Marylebone and St Pancras.[30] Such fears appeared to have a sound base in that, from the outset, the Metropolitan Police had kept a close eye on a wide range of working-class activities. The practice of 'moving on' men in the street was highly unpopular and impinged on large numbers.

The small numbers of politically active had even more grounds for concern. The revelation of police infiltration of radical groups strengthened suspicions among working-class radicals. The Select Committee claim that Sergeant Popay was acting on his own initiative in infiltrating the National Political Union and his dismissal from the force were not likely to assuage fears of police spying.[31] The policing of public demonstrations also gave rise to considerable friction. Despite the reassuring conclusion of the 1833 Select Committee into the disturbance at Cold Bath Fields, the evidence given to the Select Committee shows that many local inhabitants who witnessed the events were shocked at the brutality of the police both during and after the meeting.[32] It is unlikely that they were persuaded by the official report, which largely exonerated the police. It was a measure of popular discontent that the 5 November celebrations in 1833 saw the burning in effigy of the two Commissioners of Police, Rowan and Mayne. A guy entitled 'Justifiable Homicide', a direct reference to the coroner's verdict in the case of PC Culley, was also burnt. A popular rhyme summed up feelings:

Not a squib went fiz, nor a rocket whiz
As the Guy to the gallows was hurried
The mob were afraid of the New Police
And therefore were deucedly flurried.

Few and short were the jokes they flung
For fear of the laws did them twitch hard
But they steadfastly gazed on the Guy as he hung
And bitterly thought of Sir Richard.[33]

Even though tension may have lessened after the early troubled years, public demonstrations remained highly volatile affairs, with considerable potential for conflict between police and public. The Hyde Park Sunday Trading Riots in 1855 are a case in point. Initially there was good-natured heckling of the police. In a reference to a recent case of theft by a constable at Clerkenwell the crowd asked: 'Where are the geese? Ask the police.' But this was replaced by widespread popular condemnation following repeated police rushes into the crowd that had gathered on 1 July, the indiscriminate use of truncheons and the spectacular use of a horsewhip by Superintendent Hughes.[34]

Nor was this the last that London saw of such disturbances. In 1866/67 demonstrations in favour of electoral reform led to clashes with the police in which even Commissioner Mayne received a bloodied head. *Fun*, the satirical weekly, referred to Mayne as 'the leader of an organised gang of ruffians,' responsible for 'assaulting the Public in the execution of its duty'.[35] The booing and hissing of the police contrasted with the cheering of the military who were called in to restore order. According to a labourer who spoke to a correspondent of *The Times*, this was because 'the soldiers are men and the others ain't.... The police have no feeling for the working man; they sell themselves for 2s. a day.'[36] Again, in 1887 an attempt to ban a meeting called by the Metropolitan Radical Association to take place in Trafalgar Square as a protest against the government's failure to deal with large-scale unemployment and suffering led to violent conflict. Over 400 arrests took place and there were some 200 casualties and three fatalities. The police were criticised by *The Times* for 'striking indiscriminately in all directions,' and there were other accusations that they had meted out summary justice when told to make further arrests.[37] In retrospect the role of the police is less clear cut, but the myth of police suppression during 'Bloody Sunday' was born of pre-existing fears and helped to confirm the belief, in some quarters at least, that the police were the unequivocal defenders of the propertied against the unjustly treated and suffering propertyless.

It seems clear that incidents such as these reveal a continuing popular hostility to the police, who appeared to be agents, often enthusiastic agents, of an establishment that was unsympathetic to the demands of the politically aware working classes. However, police–public relations cannot be fully explained in these terms alone. Public demonstrations were relatively few in number, the politically active a small minority of ordinary Londoners. For the majority of working men and women their experience of the police was quite different but nonetheless profound. The introduction of the new police and the extension of police activity greatly and increasingly impinged upon their day-to-day lives.

Despite the emphasis on the primacy of crime prevention, it was clear in the first handbook issued to the Metropolitan Police, the General Instructions, that their work involved 'watching the conduct of loose and disorderly persons'.[38] Police powers regarding nuisances and petty disturbances were considerable. Writing of the impact of the wide-ranging 1822 Vagrancy Act, Roberts emphasises that 'those who, like children, adolescents and the casually employed, continued to use public space for recreation or fringe economic activity became subject to the direct discipline of the police and the magistrate's court'.[39] That discipline increased with the creation of the Metropolitan Police in 1829 and the powers were extended by the 1839 Metropolitan Police Act, while the 1867 Metropolitan Streets Act was concerned with the regulation of street trading, the systematic control of traffic and the muzzling of dogs.

Nor was this the end of the matter. On the contrary, driven by a variety of pressures from reform groups and elements in the Home Office, the Metropolitan Police's involvement in the regulation of the life of Londoners, and especially those at the lower end of the social scale, increased remorselessly. As concern was expressed about the problem of the prostitute, the habitual drunkard, the habitual vagrant, the habitual criminal, the juvenile delinquent, the gambler and the alien, so the state became more coercive and so increased police involvement in, or more accurately police intrusion into, the lives of the poor. In 1911, according to Archibald's *Metropolitan Police Guide*, there were some 643 statutes relating to police work, most of which related to the street economies or street recreations of the capital.[40]

Attempts to police morals were nothing new. Much of the concern with popular recreations stemmed from a belief they encouraged profane and immoral behaviour.[41] Cruelty to animals was no longer seen as acceptable to the new elites and they enlisted the police in their campaign to eradicate customs such as bull baiting and duck hunting. Indeed, all public gatherings were viewed with suspicion as threats to both morality and public order. Seen as nurseries of crime and hotbeds of vice, the metropolitan fairs had been under attack from the late eighteenth century onwards. Legislation passed in 1822 restricting the hours of chartered fairs and abolishing unchartered fairs could be more effectively enforced with the establishment of the Metropolitan Police in 1829. Despite their popularity, several fairs, including Bow, Tothill Fields, Edmonton and Stepney Michaelmas, were suppressed. Such actions were not universally popular. Suppression brought the risk of retaliation and the police were obvious targets for the venting of popular spleen.

However, by the mid-nineteenth century attitudes were beginning to change. The police were no longer so concerned with the threat posed by the crowd, and the actions of more respectable showmen had further reduced the concern with immorality. Such was the change that by 1843 a correspondent of *The Times*, describing Stepney fair, noted that the Commissioner of Police had no wish 'to interfere with the harmless recreations of the people at the proper seasons' and praised the police of K Division for 'the excellent arrangements ... their great forbearance and their disposition to afford every facility to the visitors'.[42] This more relaxed attitude was in evidence in the late nineteenth century. Although the police supported the abolition of Blackheath fair on the grounds of its 'great annoyance to the inhabitants of the neighbourhood who are of a highly respectable class,'[43] they played an important role in the survival of both Barnet and Pinner fairs in the 1880s and 1890s, rejecting the charges of criminality and immorality levelled at them. However, in several other respects the police became, or were perceived to become, more coercive.

Whether they approved or not, the police were increasingly expected to enforce laws directed against clearly defined outcast groups whose behaviour had been deemed to be in some way threatening to the health, security and morals of society. The police commissioners made it known that they had reservations about the police as enforcers of morals rather than fighters of crime, but in the public eye the police had a central role to play in the re-moralising of late-Victorian society and this had a corrosive effect on the public's belief in police impartiality more serious than the concerns with police partiality raised, for example, by the Sunday Trading Riots.

This can be illustrated in a number of ways. For example, the attempts to restrict prostitution, and especially the reigns of terror associated with the Contagious Diseases Acts of 1864, 1866 and 1869, greatly damaged the standing of the Metropolitan Police in those districts in which they enforced the acts with 'unabashed enthusiasm'.[44] Within London the policing of street prostitution was not unproblematic. Such was the state of the law and the nature of the market for casual sex that the police had to proceed with caution. However, pressures could be brought to bear that necessitated action. Such was the case in 1883, when a flurry of complaints to the Home Office from parish vestries and vigilance societies led Commissioner Sir Edmund Henderson to start a crusade against street prostitution which was to last for four years and which was to prove a disaster in terms of public relations for the police.[45] Allegations of the blackmailing of prostitutes and of indiscriminate arrests reached a climax with the celebrated Cass case of 1887. After a debate in Parliament and a more general condemnation of excessive police powers, the new Commissioner, Sir Charles Warren, was forced to back down. A further campaign in the early twentieth century, culminating in the d'Angely case of 1906, was almost as unsuccessful.[46] Attacks on street prostitution, like the earlier attacks on prostitution in casinos and music halls, could alienate certain sectors of the public and thus become counterproductive.[47]

The growing concern with the habitual criminal is another case in point. The habitual criminal was, in very large measure, an artificial construct brought about by three factors, all of which, singly and together, increased the likelihood of falling foul of the law and doing so on more than one occasion: the proliferation of laws and regulations, the shift in penal policy towards shorter sentences, and the greater information available to and collected by the police. However, a bogeyman was created: the habitual criminal, waging war on society. The purge on habitual criminals was limited to a relatively small number of people. However, attempts to curb drinking and gambling, through such legislation as the 1869 Wine and Beerhouses Act, the 1872 Licensing Act and the Betting Houses Acts of 1853 and 1874, brought the police into contact – and conflict – with a wider body of people. As with prostitution, many leading figures in the Met took a moderate stance on the drink question. Nonetheless, there was considerable popular anger directed at police interference in the drinking habits of ordinary Londoners. Unless under pressure from temperance and purity reformers, the police showed a reluctance to arrest drunkards unless there was a threat to public order. There was a similar ambivalence towards the habitual drunkard. The Inebriates Acts of 1888 and 1898 gave the state considerable powers in theory, if not in practice. The police saw the legislation as futile but were, nonetheless, expected to enforce it. As a consequence it was the judiciary (and to some extent public opinion), rather than the police, which emerged as the champions of the inebriate against the coercive state.[48]

Finally, attempts to control betting added to the sense of injustice at the hands of the police felt by many working men. In the last quarter of the nineteenth century gambling was increasingly seen as a major problem, threatening both the economic strength of the nation and the moral fibre of the working man. The growth of anti-betting sentiment was accelerated by the work of such pressure groups as the National Anti-Gambling League, whose propaganda received a sympathetic hearing among members of the upper echelons of the Metropolitan Police. However, the law had a clear class bias. Racecourse betting was protected by powerful forces, but not so betting in public houses or on the streets. The ordinary policeman was placed in a difficult position. Often unsympathetic to the campaign against betting, seeking to enforce unpopular and effectively unenforceable legislation, aware also that there were greater threats than gambling, he also had to face the problem of bribery.[49] As Petrow has concluded, the growing concern with the moral wellbeing of the nation and the increasingly coercive stance of the state led to a situation in which 'the Metropolitan Police were a menacing and unwelcome presence in most working-class lives'.[50] To add insult to injury, many judges and magistrates were critical of the extension of police powers and showed a concern with police behaviour and exhibited an unwillingness to find guilty on police evidence alone. Of particular concern were the practices of the expanding detection force. The need for greater supervision was an important factor in this expansion, but was fraught with difficulties. The 1877 turf fraud case revealed in spectacular fashion how detectives could be corrupted but there were other, less prominent examples of malpractice, including the taking of statements without caution and the use of third-degree tactics in interviewing, which added to popular fears and suspicions of the police.[51]

The desire to impose order and improve decorum on the streets brought reformers into conflict with the street economy of London. The costermongers interviewed by Henry Mayhew in the mid-nineteenth century had no love for the new police. As well as being responsible for a clampdown on their leisure activities such as dogfighting, they disrupted the street economy to the point of making it almost impossible to sell goods. 'Stands' or 'pitches' were banned and the costers had to carry a tray or keep moving with their barrows so as not to fall foul of the law. Intense hatred of the police was commonplace: '"Can you wonder at it, sir," said a costermonger to me, "that I hate the police? They drive us about, we must move on, we can't stand here, and we can't pitch there".' In addition, there were petty actions that created a sense of injustice and grievance. The arrest and subsequent fine of a coster, arrested when taking his dead donkey home for burial, was another example of the intervention of the 'crushers' that aroused hostility. Not surprisingly, the costers were well known for their attacks on the police. 'To serve out a policeman is the bravest act by which a costermonger can distinguish himself,' Mayhew was informed. The delight with which one boy took his revenge, inflicting a savage kicking on a constable, was not outweighed by the sentence of twelve months' imprisonment which he received. Indeed, he viewed the punishment as 'dirt cheap'.[52] Such attitudes did not die out in the mid-nineteenth century. On the contrary, growing restrictions on street trading, including the employment of young people, added new conflict points.

It is not easy to translate all these changes in police activity into more precise figures but Gatrell's recent general calculations give some indication of the impact of the greater regulation of society in the late-Victorian period. Between 1861 and 1891, a period in which rates of serious crime were falling, the ratio of arrest and summons to total population rose from one in twenty-nine to one in twenty-four for men. However, the law fell most heavily on the poor and young. The unskilled young man of London's East End probably had a one in six chance (or less) of falling foul of the law. The 'rozzers' were a constant and threatening presence for many working-class people, and mistrust and open hostility continued throughout the period under review. There is a problem with the historical evidence relating to this hostility. Official statistics of assaults on the police have to be treated with caution as a measure of anti-police sentiment, and autobiographies and oral histories may not be wholly representative. Nonetheless, there is a body of evidence that does not sit comfortably with the orthodox interpretation of the London bobby emerging as the 'handy-man of the streets' by the turn of the century.

The official statistics suggest that for the country as a whole the incidence of assaults on policemen remained high throughout the 1850s and 1860s, and peaked in the mid-1870s. Thereafter, the figures fell, although there was something of an upturn in the late 1880s and early 1890s. There were, however, important regional variations. The decline appears to have started earlier in London, dating from the late 1850s. In Manchester the fall starts in the late 1860s while in Leeds and Salford it is from the early 1870s. In Lancashire and the West Riding of Yorkshire the decline starts later still.[53]

Assaults on policemen provide an index of overt hostility to the police. While it is true that the rate of assaults on police declined in the late nineteenth century, the full significance of this fact is unclear. Society as a whole was becoming less violent and all assaults were diminishing. Furthermore, the official statistics do not necessarily measure a real change in behaviour.[54] Certainly, there was still a serious problem in the early twentieth century when some 2,500 Metropolitan policemen were injured in assaults between 1903 and 1906 alone. It would appear that something like one in four police constables were attacked each year. Not surprisingly, the cry of 'Give it to the copper' remained a common one on the streets of Victorian London.

Literary evidence points in a similar direction. Arthur Morrison's *Child of the Jago*, based on the Reverend Osborne Jay's *Life in Darkest London*, described a fictionalised Old Nichol district as one in which policemen feared to venture and in which 'to knock over two or three policemen, for kicking practice' was the delight of certain families. And such attitudes were not confined to the pages of novels. East London's H Division was notorious. The local press constantly ran stories of assaults on policemen. Policemen were kicked and, in exceptional circumstances, faced firearms.[55] Gang attacks were also not uncommon. In late June 1888, John Canavan was arrested for being drunk, disorderly and singing an indecent song in Burn Street, Limehouse. Breaking free from the arresting officer, Canavan and seventeen others stoned the constable. Later

arrested, Canavan was found guilty and fined 40s (£2) and given the
option of one month's hard labour. The persistence of anti-police
attitudes and actions is well illustrated by the case of Islington.
From the 1850s, when costers told Henry Mayhew of their hatred of
the police, which manifested itself in throwing bricks at the police
or kicking them, through to the inter-war years, when attacks on the
police, including mass rescues of people arrested, still took place,
there was limited evidence of tolerance, let alone affection, for the
police. The notorious Campbell Bunk, where flowerpots were kept
to throw at the police, was still known as 'Kill Copper Row' in the
1920s. Other oral evidence from the early twentieth century points
in the same direction. Gang attacks on the police by youths in
Edwardian England have been seen as a form of resistance to the
criminalisation of traditional street activities. Indeed, echoing some
of the problems of the recent past, it has been argued that such acts
also reflected a wider and 'profound suspicion and hostility' to the
police shared by older generations as well.[56]

It would be misleading to see anti-police sentiments simply
confined to the 'rough' or criminal elements of London society.
Many working-class people felt not simply that there was one law
for the rich and one law for the poor but also that police attention
was concentrated on the defence of better-off districts. There was a
constant undercurrent of complaint in the popular press. *Reynold's
Newspaper*, for example, was concerned with the police's pre-
occupation with petty offences, such as children's street games, and
the failure to deal with more serious crimes aroused adverse
comment. So too did high-handed and violent behaviour. It is of
more than passing interest to note that the popular culture of
London – the penny-gaffs and early music halls – had a strong anti-
police tone.

While it would be wrong to suggest that the Metropolitan Police
sought to oppress the working classes in a systematic manner, it
remains the case that their attitudes, assumptions and actions
helped to create a negative image of policing when viewed 'from
below'. Not all policemen were sympathetic to the idea of policing
morals (though they had little choice but to do so once legislation
had been passed) and some may have sympathised with the poor
and unemployed whom they had to control. But others did not. A
confidential report sent to Scotland Yard in 1904 from the
divisional inspectors and superintendents of the Metropolitan

Police clearly indicates a hostile view. The honesty and integrity of the unemployed were impugned. 'The so-called unemployed [have] the appearance of habitual loafers' while their 'poor and distressed appearance ... is due more to thriftlessness and intemperate habits than to absolute poverty'.[57] Furthermore, given the constraints on numbers, in conducting their day-to-day anti-crime role they had to make certain assumptions about likely trouble spots and likely troublemakers. This created a self-fulfilling prophecy. Areas believed to be inhabited by criminal elements, such as Jennings' Buildings, off Kensington High Street, were subject to closer scrutiny. The greater police presence, let alone the need to justify that presence, led to more arrests for criminal offences, which, in turn, confirmed the original judgement and justified continuing police surveillance. The opinions of those on the receiving end of such policing are rarely recorded but it is not difficult to see how and why suspicion, if not hatred, of the police persisted into the twentieth century.

Popular responses: the provinces

The introduction of provincial police forces was equally, if not more, problematic. In certain parts of the country there was outright opposition to the introduction of the new police. A Todmorden magistrate, writing to the Home Office in May 1840, warned that 'the very circumstances of their introduction being odious to the greater portion of our inhabitants, renders it more than probable some serious disturbance will be attempted'.[58] The events at Colne – a Chartist stronghold – provide a vivid, if exceptional, insight into the bitterness and determination with which the new police were met. The Colne force, some sixteen constables led by Superintendent Macleod, arrived in the town in mid-April 1840. Their tactics appear to have been aggressive and insensitive. Physical assaults on the populace compounded the hostility engendered by the introduction of the 'move-on system'. Open conflict broke out on 24 April, when the police were driven from the streets in what appears to have been a carefully planned operation that involved decoying the police in a town that had been thrown into darkness by the extinction of every lamp.

Superintendent Macleod was knocked out and also suffered a broken arm in the affray. The following day the town was re-occupied by twenty policemen and a new superintendent sent from Burnley. In addition, troops, both mounted and on foot, were sent to Colne on the request of the local magistrates.

The presence of the troops until the end of April ensured peace in the town. On their withdrawal the Lancashire police authorities agreed a threefold increase in the number of policemen for Colne. Saturation policing, for this is what it amounted to, succeeded and there was no rioting for almost three months. At the end of July the police presence was reduced to its initial 'normal' level. This was the signal for a fresh outbreak of trouble. The houses of known supporters of the police, most notably a local solicitor and clerk to the magistrates, Mr Bolton, were attacked and windows smashed. A more general attack on the police on 4 August saw them driven from the streets and two days later a further attack saw the police driven once again from the town. For a second time the military were ordered to the town, only to find it quiet. The troops left only to be recalled the following day after the town's dignitaries, seeking to consider how best to preserve order and property, were confronted by a group of angry Chartists. Quiet returned to Colne but when the troops withdrew after a few days there was a further upsurge of anti-police rioting on 10 August. This time the troubles resembled a civil war. On the one side were seventy special constables sworn in from the ranks of the town's 'respectable inhabitants' and the regular police whose number had been doubled by the Lancashire police authorities. On the other was a large crowd of well disciplined and armed men. In the ensuing conflict in the main streets of the town one special constable was killed as the police, yet again, were routed. Calm returned to Colne before the troops sent from Burnley arrived, but this time the authorities decided that a permanent solution had to be found. To ensure that there were no further anti-police disturbances Sir Charles Napier was ordered to establish a permanent military force, in newly built barracks, in the town.[59]

Colne was exceptional in the scale of its anti-police rioting but it was not unique. In Middleton, also in the spring of 1840, the new police were driven out of the town by a crowd incensed by the arrest of a local miner. After taking refuge in Manchester, the Middleton force was reinstated with the assistance of a large contingent of Manchester police. There was serious anti-police rioting at Lancaster races, while in the Potteries the newly created police force had to be rescued by troops and police from Liverpool. Haslingden was similarly reported to be in a state 'of great disorder because of the hostility of the populace to the police'.[60] Nor were such disturbances confined to the turbulent years of Chartism. The introduction of the West Riding Police Force in 1857 gave rise to similar disturbances.

Although less serious than the troubles in Ireland,[61] disturb-. ances also took place in several cities, such as Hull and Manchester, where the establishment of the new police had appeared more successful. In these cases the disturbances were precipitated by relatively minor brushes between police and off-duty soldiers but developed into larger-scale confrontations as members of the public took the side of the soldiers and attacked the police. A particularly striking example is afforded by Leeds. On the evening of Sunday 9 June 1844 two policemen arrested a number of soldiers of the 70th Regiment of Foot at the Green Man alehouse in York Street, following an allegation of theft and assault. Fellow soldiers attacked the police as they sought to bring the arrested men to the lock-up. More police were sent to the scene of the fight. There was nothing particularly unusual in such a set-to. Nor was it unprecedented for the troops to seek revenge on the police the following day. They set forth from the Green Parrot in Harper Street, and attacked some policemen in Vicar Lane. However, as they entered Briggate, there was a crowd, estimated at over a thousand, which responded with enthusiasm to the soldiers' cry of 'Down with the Police'. By the end of the evening four groups of civilians, including one Irish, were taking part in a series of anti-police skirmishes that resulted in the routing of the police from the centre of Leeds. The matter was resolved on the Tuesday evening when the police, regrouped and better organised, finally quelled the rioters, who were entirely drawn from local civilians.

The immediate causes of the 1844 Leeds anti-police rioting can be found in the combination of the friction between soldiers and police and the tension between magistrates and populace over the question of Sunday meetings. However, there were also longer-term causes. While the Leeds rioters were not trying to rid the city of its police, they were giving expression to anger that had built up over several years since the formation of the new police in 1836.

Certainly the local press had little doubt that the civilian rioters were motivated not 'out of love to the soldiers themselves, but from ... feelings of hatred towards the police'.[62]

The Leeds disturbances can also be seen as the most spectacular manifestation of a more general conflict between police and public that was to be found throughout the country and which persisted into the early twentieth century. In Hull in 1856 a similar incident occurred when police, attempting to arrest some soldiers for drunk and disorderly behaviour, were quickly surrounded by an angry crowd, estimated at 5,000, who facilitated the escape of the prisoners. A more serious incident took place one month later. The police were dealing with some difficulty with a major fire in the town when a company of men from HMS *Cornwallis* joined in with such effect that they had the vocal approval of the crowd that had assembled. At this point fire-hoses were turned on the sailors and a full-scale fight between them and the police broke out while the fire was ignored. Eventually the fire was put out but the incident had longer-term repercussions. Hostility towards the police continued and in the late 1860s there was a further deterioration in police–public relations. A combination of new legislation and insensitive police tactics resulted in heightened tension that culminated in the Raywell Road Riots of 1870. Allegations of high-handedness, brutality and wrongful arrest were upheld in the subsequent enquiry.[63]

Robert Roberts, writing about Salford at the turn of the century, had few illusions about the police: fear and dislike were the common responses of the poor. The autobiographical accounts of policemen bear witness to the hostility they faced. Looking back from the early 1890s, Superintendent J. Bent described being attacked, in and around Manchester, by gangs of 'scuttlers' armed with belts and buckles and even knives. On another occasion in the 1870s he was confronted by some thirty men, who wounded him with red-hot iron bars. Thomas Smethurst, a policeman in Bolton and later Stalybridge from the late 1880s to the early 1920s, faced similar threats to the person. Routine policing led to attacks by drunken men and women which occasioned beatings and kickings to various parts of the body.[64] Seemingly minor incidents could easily escalate and provide the opportunity for the local community to vent its displeasure and dislike of the police. The pages of the local press contain numerous incidents which, while having a humorous side, reveal the threats, verbal and physical, that the police had to face. When PC Purchase tried to persuade the drunken and disorderly Brigit Regan to return to her home on 'Irish Row' off Willenhall Road, Wolverhampton, on the night of 20 August 1884, he could have had little idea of the difficulties and dangers that were to ensue. On several occasions he persuaded the women indoors to let her in, only for her to return outside and continue the disturbance. With the door kept closed for five minutes Purchase appeared to have succeeded when Regan reappeared and attacked him with a poker. With PC Thompson in assistance an attempt was made to take the woman into custody. Unfortunately, by this time a hostile crowd, estimated at 1,500, had assembled. The two constables were attacked and dragged into Regan's house where they were held several hours, during which time they were 'maltreated by the mob'.[65] In this instance the men do not appear to have been severely injured, but this was not always the case.

In Middlesbrough in January 1865 there were two major incidents which highlighted the strength of anti-police feeling in some quarters of the town. In the first a crowd of about 500 people assaulted PC Wilkinson and freed a man, Peter Evans, who had been under arrest. In the second, a smaller gang set upon PC Stainsby, beating, biting and kicking him. Similar incidents continued in the town throughout the period. After a brief respite in the 1880s, there was an upsurge in attacks in the 1890s and especially the 1900s. For example, in February 1905 there were 'hooligan' attacks on PCs Goddard and Dobson, while three men were arrested for giving PC Barker a severe kicking. Nor were the assaults inflicted solely by men. In January 1910 PC Bate was able to return to work after several weeks on sick leave following an assault in which he was 'viciously kicked in the stomach' by Annie Lee. The motives behind such attacks are not always clear but it is evident that in many cases dislike of the police in general and/or hatred of individual policemen in particular played a part. Middlesbrough, once again, provides a graphic example. On Christmas Eve 1919 Inspector Burney and PC Bainbridge were coming off duty only to be met by a 'drunken mob'. Burney was kicked to death and Bainbridge forced to retire as a result of the injuries he sustained. The incident, however, was a case of mistaken identity. The unfortunate Burney had been mistaken for the much-hated Inspector Sowerby, who had built up a reputation for aggressiveness in a career that had spanned many years in the town.[66]

Further examples can be quoted. In Birmingham anti-police disturbances were particularly frequent in the 1830s and 1840s, and again in the 1870s, the latter due to the enforcement of licensing laws and harsh Poor Law policies. Non-co-operation and a 'steady mistrust and dislike of the police' were the response of the working-class community. Indeed, for some time, parts of the city, such as the area behind the Theatre Royal, were effectively no-go areas for the new police. The Navigation Street gang effectively controlled this particular area until the time of the riots in Navigation Street, during which a policeman was killed, when the authorities asserted their control.[67]

Also in the Midlands, Northampton experienced three major riots, involving anti-police violence, between 1854 and 1878. The riot of 1854 and the 'militia' riot of 1878 both stemmed from conflicts between soldiers and police. The arrest of William Gay of the Royal Artillery on a charge of theft in the summer of 1854 led to a crowd of about 300 rescuing the prisoner. Truncheon-wielding constables recaptured their man but a rumour that Gay had been murdered by the police led to an escalation of trouble. The Riot Act was read at 10 p.m. on the evening of 14 August. Notwithstanding the support of the local militia and, ironically, a detachment of Royal Artillery men, the streets were not cleared until 2 a.m. the following morning. A crowd assembled later on the Tuesday evening and at 10 p.m. the Riot Act was read again. This time the crowd was dispersed more quickly and there were only desultory disturbances the following day.

The 1878 riot also took place on a summer evening and was sparked off by another rumour of the death of a militiaman at the hands of the police. A crowd of over 100 civilians and some members of the militia attacked members of the borough police force. By 11 p.m., one hour after the reading of the Riot Act, order was restored. However, for the next three days, 3–5 June, there were running fights between the police and crowds in the town centre. The third disturbance, the Bradlaugh riot, was political in origin. It took place in 1874 and involved a crowd estimated at 7,000. With only fifty regulars and twenty specials, the police suffered several serious injuries as political passions turned into anti-police violence.[68]

However, it would be wrong to imply that anti-police tensions were a serious problem across all urban England. Despite some assaults on police there appears to have been no serious problems to be found in York following the advent of the new police. Similarly, there was no great dislike of the police in Southampton, while in Portsmouth the new police were viewed with 'mild curiosity'. Furthermore, in many towns the police forces were too small and inefficient to make a major impact and this in itself lessened the likelihood of tension.[69]

It would also be misleading to suggest that anti-police violence was simply an urban phenomenon. It was certainly to be found in the countryside. When PC Thomas Griffiths, one of 'Paddy Mayne's Grasshoppers' in Shropshire, visited the Old Three Pigeons, a public house in Nesscliff, on New Year's Eve, 1841, he was met with a hostile crowd of locals. He was lifted into the air and thrown into the fire, from whence he escaped, only to be further assaulted and kicked under a cupboard. The intervention of the landlady enabled him to reach safety in the cellar but it was a further three months before he was fit enough to appear before the local magistrates. Rural constables could find themselves identified as 'a landowners' lackey' as they became embroiled in the poaching wars that rumbled on for much of the nineteenth century. Worse, as in the case of the Hungerford murders of 1877, they could be killed.[70]

More common were the assaults that followed arrests. In 1871 the Wimborne petty sessions dealt with a case in which six men – three of them confusingly named Zebedee – were tried for assaulting two constables. It had taken the police three-quarters of an hour to bring their prisoners, kicking and biting, 100 yards to the gaol. PC Richard Hann, involved in this incident, was assaulted on at least seven occasions between 1860 and 1882 by a variety of men and women, including a retired sailor with a wooden leg! In parts of Warwickshire the defence of traditional leisure activities led to attacks on the police while in Bedfordshire older forms of protest were to be seen. Two unpopular policemen in Eaton Bray were subjected to rough music after the sentencing of eight men following assaults on the village policemen. Similarly, the highly unpopular PC Enoch Raison came into such conflict with the inhabitants of Stebbing, Essex, that they threatened to run him out of the village. On 5 November he was burnt in effigy in a public display of communal disapproval. An attempt to smuggle him out of the village failed and the unfortunate man left to a shower of catcalls and missiles. Such overt action was highly unusual but rumbling discontent could be found near the surface. Speaking more generally about attitudes in the late nineteenth century, Billy Dixon, a Norfolk farm labourer, noted how the police were 'against the population then in them days'.[71] But again, one must not exaggerate the extent of opposition. Rural populations were more scattered and the police often adopted a wait-and-see policy, which minimised conflict. As a consequence there was less open hostility, though there may have been considerable non-co-operation.[72]

These responses to the new police grew out of the resentment felt at the general, day-to-day nature of police work and the way in which it was conducted. More specifically, police interest in popular recreation and leisure activities and their handling of industrial disputes were particularly contentious.

The concern with plebeian customs and recreations predated the advent of the new police by many decades. However, as the attack on popular leisure gathered pace in the early and mid-nineteenth century, the police became allies, willing or otherwise, of re-formers. The use of the police is well documented. In the Black Country the newly formed Staffordshire County Police Force was used to crack down on 'popular and rowdy recreations' such as wakes and fairs and various forms of animal baiting and fighting.[73] Such was the unpopularity of the police as they arrested people attending prize fights or at other illegal gatherings that there was an increase in the number of minor riots in the mid-1840s as constables were assaulted and prisoners rescued. In addition, there were many prosecutions for assaulting the police, a further indication of their unpopularity. Nor was such unpopularity confined to the Black Country in the 1840s. Arrests at the Oldham wakes in the mid-1860s led to similar anti-police attacks. Interestingly, the local paper, the *Oldham Gazette*, was critical of the police for their actions in seeking to arrest people for petty offences.

The pattern of change was not uniform across the country. The virulence with which certain traditions were defended in parts of the country and the determination with which authorities acted to stamp them out created real tensions between the proponents of old and new cultures. In Birmingham in the early 1830s there was a determined attempt by magistrates and the newly formed police to eradicate cockfighting. In one incident forty spectators were arrested, tied in pairs with rope and paraded through the town. Public humiliation was added to prosecution as a deterrent.[74]

Perhaps the most spectacular defence of popular custom took place at Stamford, where the local bull-run survived well into the mid-nineteenth century. Having survived a series of attacks in the late eighteenth century, the bull-run came under renewed pressure from reformers in the 1830s. In 1839 the issue came to a climax. The bull-run had been declared illegal by the Court of Queen's Bench in 1838 and, by way of preparation for the extirpation of this 'barbarous practice', forty-three dragoons and twenty Metropolitan policemen were despatched to Stamford to reinforce the ninety local policemen. Despite such numbers the police failed to prevent a bull being smuggled into the town and run through the streets. Only the arrival of the dragoons prevented a second bull being run. The bullards' victory was a Pyrrhic one. Such was the cost of preventive actions that in 1840 a concerted effort mounted by the worthies of Stamford, and without outside assistance, brought about the ending of the custom.[75]

The Stamford incident is a useful corrective to the belief that reformers, aided and abetted by the new police, swept all before them. Similarly, Guy Fawkes celebrations in southern England survived in their traditional form until the late nineteenth century. While there is debate as to the precise nature of these events, there is little doubt that the attempts to prevent fires taking place brought conflict between police and some of the public. Attempts to stop the celebrations in Horncastle in 1838 saw the two local policemen forced to retreat to a local house under a shower of horse dung, bricks and stones. In Witham there were serious disturbances on at least nine occasions in the thirty years before 1890. In 1873 the police succeeded in preventing the fire, but at a cost. In the riot that took place two constables were injured. Even the presence of the chief constable, as in 1881, could not prevent friction turning into riot. At Guildford in 1843 police intervention provoked a violent reaction that saw the home of the super-intendent of police attacked and damaged. Indeed, such were the dangers on 5 November that the police were locked in their station and given beer and bread by the superintendent![76] Matters came to a climax in the 1860s. In a concerted effort to stamp out the celebrations the police strength in the town was increased by some two-thirds and augmented by specials. On the eve of Boxing Day a riot instigated by the 'town guys' organising the celebrations saw a policeman severely beaten and left for dead. Subsequent arrests and imprisonments finally brought the popular resistance to an end.

Elsewhere, Nuneaton folk-football survived until the late nineteenth century. In 1881 E. H. Coleman noted 'the police attempted to stop the game, but were somewhat roughly handled'. The Whittlesey 'straw bears' survived Victoria's reign to be finally forbidden in 1905 by a 'zealous inspector of police'.[77] Such triumphs were not universally welcomed. The demise of the 'straw bears' was seen as a triumph for bumbledom while the police-precipitated loss of traditional recreations in Batley was lamented by men such as John Binns. Writing in 1882, he had no doubts about the role of the local police in the demise of local customs. He noted how:

> the first policeman came into our midst, to plant the thin edge of the wedge which was to revolutionize our manners and customs ... we have lost all traces of mummery; all traces of Lee Fair ... most of our Mischief Night; as nearly all the peace eggers; for what are left of the latter are of another mould to those of my childhood days.... If mummers were to be seen upon the street now, the police would interfere. I put a deal of this severance from ourselves of old customs down to the advent of the policeman in uniform.[78]

It is debatable to what extent instances of violence against police were simply defences of traditional sports and recreations. There is a sense in which the defence of a 'rough', rather than 'respectable', culture re-created itself as leisure activities were modernised. New sports, notably association football, were associated with violence, including attacks upon policemen.[79]

Public houses and beer shops were also subject to close scrutiny. The reasons for this are not hard to find. Many Victorian experts believed that there was a direct link between drink and crime. Others were concerned with the spread of seditious ideas to the unsuspecting poor as the result of clandestine meetings held at such venues. And yet others were concerned with the general immorality and profanity of leisure activities based on the pub. Police powers were increased by the 1869 Wine and Beerhouses Act and the 1872 Licensing Act. The surveillance of pub-based activities and the 'moving on' of men outside beer houses led to friction. In exceptional circumstances, such as the Leeds incident noted above, there could be serious disturbances. More common were minor fracas, arrests for drunk and disorderly behaviour, possibly crowd disturbances as attempts were made to rescue prisoners and more commonly a sense of resentment that traditional leisure activities were being scrutinised and disrupted. While it is almost certainly the case that the presence of the police became part of the normal order of daily life and 'police interference' was seen more as part of their routine, one should not minimise the tenacity with which mistrust and dislike continued in many working-class communities. The police had clearly become a permanent feature of life, but begrudging acquiescence more accurately sums up the popular response to this fact.

As in London, the new police found themselves in conflict with the street traders and shopkeepers in provincial towns and cities as public space came under increasing control. For example, the 1841 Middlesbrough Improvement Act, which made provision for the appointment of town constables, contained detailed provisions that covered all aspects of trading in the town. Barrows could be left standing only for the time it took to load or unload. Thereafter, the owner was liable to a fine of £2. Shopkeepers displaying wares in a manner that obstructed the footpaths or inconvenienced pedestrians were liable to a similar fine. In Rochdale the advent of the new police brought a similar purge on peddlers and street sellers.[80] Much attention has been focused on the 1830s and 1840s, when the novelty of such action was greatest, but it should not be overlooked that, although familiarity might have lessened some of the tension between police and street traders, the scope of police involvement in urban street economies increased over the course of the nineteenth century. Moreover, as police forces increased in size and efficiency, their impact also was greater.

Although directly affecting a smaller percentage of the population, industrial disputes provided some of the most bitter and highly publicised confrontations between police and public. Police involvement, whether seeking to maintain order at time of riot or escorting 'free labour', laid them open to the charge of partisanship. Whatever justification might be given, the police no longer appeared to be impartial but were very visibly the agents of employers and their allies. The mid to late nineteenth century furnishes several examples.

Lancashire witnessed many scenes of violence. A strike in Wigan in 1853 led to rioting that was exacerbated by the arrival of the police. Their close identification with employers, which was a major cause of the hostility, was demonstrated most clearly during the cotton famine of 1863, when a local mill owner in Ashton, Hugh Mason, was carried on the shoulders of two policemen as a warning to the crowd. Similarly, Richard Jervis, recounting his experience of policing a strike in Bolton, noted the 'generous manner in which they [the police] were treated by the Town Council and the foundry masters at whose works they were posted'.[81]

During the bitter nine-week strike in the north Lancashire cotton district in 1878, there were several reported riots which involved attacks on the police in such towns as Accrington, Blackburn, Burnley and Preston. In the last the police found themselves facing a hail of herrings and oranges! In one of the worst incidents, at Darwen, there was a collapse in law and order that lasted for several days. At its worst on 10 May, police reinforcements, who had been called in from Blackburn, Bolton, Burnley, Clitheroe and Manchester, were attacked by a crowd estimated to be in excess of 2,000, while the police station also came under siege. The Chief Constable of Lancashire was one of the victims, cut by a stone. Allegations of police brutality heightened tensions with the strikers and on the following day in circumstances that were close to guerrilla warfare in the town the Deputy Chief Constable was laid low by a missile. Undoubtedly the particular circumstances of a bitter strike were an important and immediate element in the anti-police actions, but there was a long-standing underlying hostility to the police that also fuelled the attacks. Such troubles recurred later in the century. In 1881 the police, armed with cutlasses, fought miners in what became known as the Battle of Howe Bridge. However, in contrast, during the 1893 miners' strike in Leigh, the police opened soup kitchens and fed hundreds of people in a gesture that won much local approval.[82]

Some of the worst disturbances took place in the coalfields of South Wales, where the police had taken an overt stance against political radicals and trade unionists since the late 1830s. At that time the Chief Constable of Glamorgan had intervened to get local iron masters to dismiss alleged extremists. By the early twentieth century, growing social polarisation, intensifying economic constraints on employers and stagnating, if not falling, real wages for employees gave rise to a highly volatile situation in South Wales. The situation was exacerbated by a clear identification of interests between colliery owners and police chiefs that dated back to the early 1890s. The Chief Constable of Glamorgan, Captain Lionel Lindsay, took a very simple view of matters: there was a threat from socialist subversives that had to be dealt with firmly and forcefully. The situation was confused by the introduction of Metropolitan Police under the command of General Macready. Macready, during his brief stay in South Wales, sought to translate into reality the Home Office's utterances on impartiality. He was prepared to negotiate with the strikers and to allow peaceful picketing by small numbers, and so Macready distanced himself from the employers. The police were not to be an intimidatory force to be used at their beck and call. Indeed, Macready went further and even criticised, albeit with no effect, the employers' use of scab labour. Despite the attempt to bring an alternative form of strike policing, there were major problems. The Metropolitan Police were unpopular and there were accusations in the local press not only from strikers but also from local tradesmen and clerics of indiscriminate baton charges and other police brutalities.[83]

The transport strikes of 1911 also brought some major disturbances, most notably Liverpool's 'Bloody Sunday', 13 August 1911. Police had been brought in from Birmingham and Leeds to clear the streets of strikers – a policy that had the approval of Winston Churchill at the Home Office. Police attacked the largest demonstration held in the city and precipitated two days of rioting, in which two people were killed and many more injured. However, violence was not the inevitable outcome, as events in Hull demonstrated. Despite the pressure for strong action by the city's influential ship owners (who also had the backing of Churchill), the local watch committee acted cautiously and was prepared to offer police protection only if a breach of the peace seemed imminent. Furthermore, the offer of outside police help was refused in a deliberate attempt to prevent the situation overheating. Finally, unlike Lindsay in Glamorgan, the Chief Constable of Hull adopted a more conciliatory line and there was none of the rioting and anti-police disturbances that had taken place elsewhere.

Where violence took place this had the effect of confirming pre-existing animosities. During the dockers' strike, Robert Roberts witnessed a neighbour struck on the head by a mounted police officer. The blow, 'like the thump of wood on a swede turnip,' left the man incapable of work and evidently brain damaged for life. As Roberts concluded, with resignation as much as bitterness, 'the actions of the police during these troublesome times had left them no better loved than they had been before'.[84] Elsewhere bitterness was more apparent, as in a parody of 'The Charge of the Light Brigade' which appeared in the *Sunderland Daily Echo* in 1891, following police action in the town:

> Pounding at ev'ry head
> Quiet folks' blood was shed;
> Women and children
> Reeled from the blows that sped,
> Moaning and sundered.
> Then they marched back again
> Gallant Half Hundred![85]

It is also important to look at the racial dimension of policing. There is abundant evidence from virtually every part of the country to show that a disproportionate number of Irish men and women found themselves in court. In England and Wales as a whole, Irish-born offenders accounted for 12–15 per cent of all committals between 1861 and 1891 and, although this figure fell to below 10 per cent in the early twentieth century, these figures represent a fivefold over-representation of the Irish. The percentage of Irish-born offenders arrested in certain towns was substantial: over a third in Liverpool in 1861 and 1871; above a quarter in Preston from 1861 to 1891; and ranging from a fifth to just under a third in Bradford and Manchester in 1861 and 1871. In all cases the Irish-born were heavily over-represented. In the worst case, that of Preston, over-representation rose from a factor of three to over eight. A similar situation was to found in York, while in Birmingham the over-representation of Irish-born people accused of assaulting the police was extremely high. To some extent this was the product of prevailing attitudes and policing practices. The stereotype of the drunken, violent and criminally inclined Irishman was well established in nineteenth-century England. It was also the case that the closer surveillance of working-class districts by the new police made the Irish particularly vulnerable. In Leeds, Bradford, Manchester, Wolverhampton, as well as in London, 'Little Irelands' were singled out as problem areas, to be dealt with accordingly. At times such policing was almost paramilitary in nature and it is hardly surprising, therefore, to find that assaults on policemen by Irish men and women were above average for England as a whole. What is more many of the instances involved large-scale conflicts, with many members of the local Irish community rallying to protect or rescue one of their own. The superintendent of the night watch in Manchester in 1830 observed:

It repeatedly happens that, in order to apprehend one Irishman in the Irish parts of the town, we are forced to take from ten or twenty, or even more, watchmen. The whole neighbourhood will turn out with weapons, even women, half-naked, carrying brickbats and stones for the men to throw. A man will resist, fighting and struggling, in order to gain time till his friends collect for a rescue, so that he has scarcely a rag left upon him when he is brought to the lock-up.[86]

The Irish were prominent in many of the disturbances in the Black Country in the 1850s, while in Middlesbrough in the 1860s and 1870s there were repeated cases of large-scale assaults and rescues as the police sought to arrest Irishmen living 'over the border' in the old town centre. In the autumn of 1864 Superintendent Saggerson drew the attention of the watch committee to 'an increase of fifty-seven assaults on the police arising out of the opposition [by the lowest class of Irish people] to the Constables when endeavouring in the execution of their duty to check disorderly conduct and preserve the peace'. Assaults continued and early in the new year PC Stainsby attempted to arrest a labourer, Michael Lougheran,

who commenced kicking the officer and striking him, [while another] four or five men came up and assisted him in committing a most brutal assault. The officer was knocked down and the men attacked him in the most savage manner kicking him with their feet, striking him with sticks which they carried with them and biting him. Two severe wounds were inflicted on the top of his head and the officer was rendered well-nigh insensible. [87]

In the same month a more serious incident took place. Patrick Evans, referred to as 'an Emeralder' in the local newspaper, had been arrested for assault, including an attack on PC Wilkinson. 'The officer then took him into custody, when the prisoner called on the crowd to liberate him. Several of his comrades and the prisoner commenced to beat and kick the officer who was presently surrounded by a crowd of 500 to 600 people.' Further incidents occurred in 1866 and 1867; a shift in sentencing policy by local magistrates – convicted offenders were sent to gaol without the option of a fine – seems to have reduced the number but the problem rumbled on. Almost a decade later, in November 1875, six 'low Irishmen' were arrested for an attack on Sergeant Raisbeck. As the *Middlesbrough Weekly News* disapprovingly recognised, for at least one section of the local community the police were seen as enemies and associated with tyranny.[88]

The disproportionate number of Irishmen involved in crimes, and especially assaults on the police, cannot be explained simply in terms of police hostility, even though they often accepted contemporary stereotypes, which were couched in crude racist terms, that depicted the Irish as an inferior and criminally prone race. However, it was also the case that the Irish, for the most part, were recent arrivals with little or no experience of the 'respectable' English standards that were being enforced by the new police, nor of the self-discipline of English workers. Furthermore, insofar as they had experience of policing in Ireland, they viewed the police as a hostile and alien force and did not recognise their legitimacy to the same degree as some, though not all, of the English working classes.

Finally, reference must be made to the positive responses to the police. The 'soup kitchen' side of their work often brought genuine gratitude. So to did their work in emergencies. Dealing with runaway animals, fires and floods, many policemen put their lives at risk to save or help the public, and this did not go without recognition. For example, after the Norfolk floods of August 1912, there were a number of brave rescue actions, one of which involved a policeman and a local boatman bringing some 100 people to safety. The local press commented on police actions in the following words:

> Day and night they have been at their posts, and have cheerfully undertaken tasks that lie beyond the scope of their recognised duties ... [A]t the height of the flood [they] rendered yeomen service in

rescuing, pacifying and removing to places of shelter numberless wretched, half-drowned men, women and children and all this was done with a gentleness and solicitude for their welfare and comfort that won the gratitude of the affected ones.[89]

Conclusion

The orthodox emphasis on the widespread and rapid acceptance of the police is a misleading oversimplification, but it does contain an important element of truth that has been overlooked in certain recent writings. By the early twentieth century the police as police were recognised as a permanent feature of everyday life. There was also a wider degree of acceptance of the police than fifty years before. The fact that England was a less impoverished, less divided and more 'respectable' society than it had been in the 1840s made the task of policing easier and the police less unacceptable. However, the evidence from Victorian and Edwardian England does not unequivocally support the optimistic interpretations of early police historians such as Reith and Critchley. Their view is partial and misleading. While middle- and upper-class support may well have been gained from an early stage in the second quarter of the nineteenth century (and even this is an over-simplification, as the concern about excessive police powers shown by journalists and the judiciary indicates), the same cannot be said about the working classes. Given the diversity of the country's economy and society one cannot talk of a single working-class response and even divisions into 'rough' and 'respectable' attitudes can be misleading. However, a number of conclusions can be offered.

First, working-class opposition to the new police was wide-spread, extending beyond the 'rough' and criminal elements and beyond the ranks of organised labour and the politically active. The very nature of policing meant that many ordinary men and women were likely to come into contact and conflict with the law in the course of their daily work and leisure. As Reynolds and the Woolleys observed in 1911:

Whether or not he [the working man] comes into collision with them [the police] is more a matter of good fortune than law-abidingness, and he is a lucky man who does not find himself in their hands at one time or another in his life.[90]

Second, the extension of police work into yet more sensitive areas of daily life probably extended and deepened contact and hostility in the late nineteenth and early twentieth centuries. The likelihood of arrest increased in the last third of the nineteenth century and for certain more marginalised groups, then as now, there was a very high chance of receiving a summons or being arrested. Moreover, many infractions of the law involved a conflict of values:

> The police are charged not only with the prevention and detection of crime ... but with the enforcement of a whole mass of petty enactments which are little more than social regulations bearing almost entirely on working-class life ... the duties of the police have been made to tally with upper-class, as opposed to working-class, notions of right and wrong.[91]

From this it followed that for many ordinary men and women the most common perception of the policeman was of an agent of a different class, seeking to enforce his values in matters which, however socially reprehensible, were hardly threatening to the fabric of society. As Flora Thompson noted, even law-abiding people with 'no personal reason for fearing the police' viewed 'the village constable as a potential enemy, set to spy upon them by the authorities.'[92]

Third, conflict was exacerbated by incompetent, insensitive and even corrupt policing. The 'irksomeness of their arbitrary rulings' meant that they were viewed, especially in the early days, as 'oppressors and obnoxious outsiders'.[93] Further, the police were as much, if not more, accepted because of the force they had at their disposal than for being the embodiment of an abstract concept of justice that protected all, irrespective of class, against those who broke the law and threatened the peace and security of society. But conflict was reduced by operational constraints born of an awareness of the limitations of police powers (and a reluctance of ordinary policemen to enforce all legislation and regulations with enthusiasm). Limitations of manpower meant that not only did priorities have to be set by the police but also that these priorities had, in the long run, to gain the acquiescence of a majority of the policed. To that extent, the police were constrained by the policed.

Fourth, the ideologically important crime-fighting role of the police (probably given an exaggerated importance by the general decline in theft and serious crime in the latter part of the century) brought benefits to the working classes, albeit to a lesser degree than to the middle and upper classes, which created a more positive image of the police, which was enhanced by the determination of successive police commissioners and provincial chief constables to develop and stress the public service role of the force. Furthermore, the operation of the police courts further added to the belief that there was a system of justice for working people too.[94] However, a growing confidence in the law did not necessarily bring a corresponding increase in respect for the police.

Fifth, contrary to the revisionist interpretation, there is clear evidence of co-operation between public and police increasing over the years and also of genuine affection developing in certain instances. When PC Stephens of the Leicester police died in 1908, thousands lined the streets for his funeral procession and there seems to have been a widespread and genuine grief at the loss of a respected figure.[95]

Sixth, even when positive acceptance did not exist, there was a begrudging acceptance that the police were an established part of life, but this fragile toleration could easily break down, especially at times of political and industrial crisis, when the police were clearly seen as agents of an elite which sought to impose its beliefs and behaviour upon others.

Finally, one must stress the variable nature and success of the police presence and the complexity of popular response. To see the police simply as agents of social control is seductive but misleading. The concept of social control is itself problematic.[96] Used uncritically to explain all state actions, it ends up explaining nothing. This is not to suggest that there was not a widespread concern among Victorian ruling elites about the threat from below, nor that these people took a variety of actions, direct and indirect, to maintain their control of power through the creation or enforcement of common codes of behaviour. More specifically, because the policed were predominantly drawn from the working classes, the police were widely viewed as agents of the propertied classes. However, attitudes changed over time. By the late nineteenth century it was less common to equate the working classes as a whole with the dangerous classes. Certain groups were singled out for close attention, particularly when they impinged upon respectable society, but other groups were only lightly policed. Moreover, policing itself involved a more varied series of functions and necessarily had a more complex impact than revisionists allow.

Not surprisingly, popular responses varied considerably between and within classes. Furthermore, individual responses were rarely constant or consistent. In one circumstance, the policeman was a genial figure, returning a lost child; in another, a welcome defender against petty thieves. But equally, he could be the heavy-handed figure, brusquely enforcing laws and even applying punishments to activities that did not appear to be either sinful or threatening. Worse still, he could be a brutal threat to rights as he escorted scab labour to work during a strike. The multi-faceted nature of police work, let alone the immense variability of the police as a body of men, meant that there was no single or simple experience of policing and, therefore, no single or simple response. The 'bobby' appeared to be, and indeed was, a complex and contradictory figure who defied simple classification.[97]

Notes

1   Cited in C. Reith, *A New Study of Police History*, London, Oliver & Boyd, 1956, p. 135.

2   *Ibid.*, p. 136.

3   *Ibid.*, p. 135.

4 ·   R. D. Storch, 'The plague of blue locusts: police reform and popular resistance in northern England, 1840–1857', *International Review of Social History*, 20, 1975.

5   The following is based on the extracts from the guidance given to Birmingham's constables in 1839. Cited in A. H. Manchester, *Sources of English Legal History, 1750–1950*, London, Butterworths, 1984, pp. 248–50.

6   General order, 25 May 1836, cited in B. D. Butcher, '*A Movable, Rambling Force': An Official History of Policing in Norfolk*, Norwich, Norfolk Constabulary, 1989, p. 10.

7   These details are taken at random from the tables appended to the annual reports of the Chief Constable of Middlesbrough for the year 1907/8.

Cleveland County Archive, CB/M/C, 1/68. A similar pattern of development can be seen in other towns. Increased police responsibilities in Oldham are detailed in D. Taylor, *999 And All That*, Oldham, Oldham Corporation, 1968, chapter 8.

8 C. Steedman, *Policing the Victorian Community: The Formation of English Provincial Police Forces, 1856–80*, London, Routledge and Kegan Paul, 1984, p. 159.

9 The corollary of this was the belief that there was a majority of inherently peaceable and law-abiding people who accepted the police as defenders of order. This was shown to be problematic in the late nineteenth century, when police involvement in industrial disputes increased and one-time peaceable citizens often became violently opposed to the police.

10 Leeds City Council in 1836 sought to defend the Sabbath against profanity by clamping down on Sunday sports and drinking. Leeds' 1842 Improvement Act gave the police powers to prosecute the owners of public houses in which cockfighting and the like took place. Similarly, cockfighting, dogfighting, bull baiting and badger baiting were expressly banned by the Council in Manchester in 1843. R. D. Storch, 'The policeman as domestic missionary', *Journal of Social History*, 9, 1976. Bye-laws in Huddersfield and Hull restricted the times during which rugs and carpets could be shaken in the streets while the Middlesbrough Improvement Act prohibited the discarding of orange peel on the flags.

11 In Middlesbrough in 1855, 851 people were dealt with, of whom only forty-six were tried for serious offences. For the remainder the most common charges related to drunkenness and assault but there was a wide range of summary prosecutions for obstructing the footpath, using foul language and so forth. D. Taylor, 'Crime and policing in early Victorian Middlesbrough, 1835–55', *Journal of Local and Regional Studies*, 11, 1991.

12 M. Hann, *Policing Victorian Dorset*, Wincanton, Dorset Publishing, 1989, pp. 76–87. Butcher, *Movable, Rambling Force*, p. 13.

13 Cited in M. Brogden, *The Police: Autonomy and Consent*, London, Academic Press, 1982, p. 67.

14 R. Swift, *Police Reform in Early Victorian York, 1835–1856*, University of York, Borthwick Papers, no. 73, 1988, pp. 26–7.

15 Storch, 'Domestic missionary', pp. 484–5, 490. Heaton was a zealous reader of old statutes and resurrected pieces of legislation which had long been in disuse, as in this case.

16 Mr Sadler to Select Committee on County Rates, *Parliamentary Papers*, 1850, xiii, pp. 199–200, cited in Steedman, *Policing*, p. 140.

17 For the Middlesbrough police, including Superintendent Saggerson, it made sense to minimise conflict in a town that saw several vicious assaults on the police.

18 J. Davis, 'From "rookeries" to "communities": race, poverty and policing in London, 1850–1985', *History Workshop Journal*, 14, 1987.

19 A. A. Clarke, *Country Coppers: The Story of the East Riding Police*, Arton Books, Hornsea, 1993, p. 25. The question of police violence is a vexed one. Translating the theory of 'minimal force' into practice is not straightforward. While it is the case that English police were not heavily armed – the carrying of cutlasses and guns was rare – it is also important to note that the baton was intended to be a disabling instrument. In theory the use of the baton was limited but internal codes of behaviour among ordinary constables probably gave quasi-legitimacy to actions that were frowned upon by seniors. The extent to which the police used batons and rolled capes, not to mention boots and fists, against 'ordinary' members of the public is unknowable. Complaints of police brutality recur throughout the period but the unreliability of the evidence makes it very difficult to determine the level or degree of such actions over time.

20 For a highly critical view see J. J. Tobias, *Crime and Industrial Society in the Nineteenth Century*, London, Penguin, 1973, especially the appendix. A more positive view is taken in V. A. C. Gatrell and T. B. Hadden, 'Criminal statistics and their interpretation', in E. A. Wrigley, ed., *Nineteenth Century Society*, Cambridge, Cambridge University Press, 1972; V. A. C. Gatrell, 'The decline of theft and violence in Victorian and Edwardian England', in V. Gatrell, B. Lenman and G. Parker, eds, *Crime and the Law*, London, Europa, 1980; and D. Philips, *Crime and Authority in Victorian England*, London, Croom Helm, 1977, chapter 2.

21 Gatrell, 'Decline', p. 281, points to a 43 per cent decline in the rate of indictable offences between the early 1860s and the 1890s.

22 *Ibid.*; D. J. V. Jones, *Crime, Protest, Community and Police*, London, Routledge and Kegan Paul, 1982.

23 Gatrell, 'Decline', p. 259.

24 B. Davey, *Lawless and Immoral: Policing a Country Town, 1835–1857*, Leicester, Leicester University Press, 1983, p. 182.

25 M. Weaver, 'The new science of policing: crime and the Birmingham Police Force, 1839–1842', *Albion*, 26, 1994.

26 *Liverpool Mercury*, 11 March 1836, cited in Brogden, *The Police*, p. 49; Swift, *Police Reform*, p. 36; R. D. Storch, 'Policing rural southern England before the police: opinion and practice, 1830–1856', in D. Hay and F. Synder, eds, *Policing and Prosecution in Britain, 1750–1850*, Oxford, Oxford University Press, 1989.

27 For changing attitudes towards male violence and attempts to limit it by law see M. E. Doggett, *Marriage, Wife-Beating and the Law in Victorian England*, London, Weinfeld & Nicholson, 1992; and M. S. Shanley, *Feminism, Marriage and the Law in Victorian England, 1850–1895*, London, Taurus, 1989. B. Caine, *Victorian Feminists*, Oxford, Oxford University Press, 1992, has a useful introductory chapter on Frances Power Cobbe, whose work is discussed in C. Bauer and L. Ritt, '"A husband is a beating animal": Frances Power Cobbe confronts the wife-abuse problem in Victorian England',

International Journal of Women's Studies, 6, 1989. See also E. Ross, '"Fierce questions and taunts": married life in working-class London', *Feminist Studies*, 8, 1982; and N. Tomes, '"A torrent of abuse": crimes of violence between working-class men and women in London', *Journal of Social History*, 11, 1978.

28 C. Reith, *A Short History of the Police*, Oxford, Oxford University Press, 1948, pp. 44, 49, 60; T. A. Critchley, *A History of Police in England and Wales*, London, Constable, 1979, p. 56.

29 W. Miller, 'London's police tradition in a changing society', in S. Holdaway, ed., *The British Police*, London, Edward Arnold, 1979, p. 19.

30 Storch, 'Plague', p. 68.

31 Report of the Select Committee on the Petition of Frederick Young and Others, *Parliamentary Papers*, 1833 (627), xiii.

32 Report of the Select Committee on the Cold Bath Fields Meeting, 1833, *Parliamentary Papers*, 1833 (718), xiii. See the evidence of Nathaniel Stallwood, especially QQ 266, 311, 317, 350–1; James Brown Q 630 and John Hudson QQ 736–46.

33 Cited in R. D. Storch, 'Please to remember the fifth of November: conflict, solidarity and public order in southern England, 1815–1900', in R. D. Storch, ed., *Popular Culture in Nineteenth Century Britain*, London, Croom Helm, 1982, p. 80.

34 P. T. Smith, *Policing Victorian London*, Connecticut, Greenwood Press, 1985, chapter 6; and *Parliamentary Debates*, 3rd series, 139, 1855, cols 368–463.

35 *Fun*, 4 August 1866, cited in C. Emsley, *The English Police: A Political and Social History*, Hemel Hempstead, Harvester Wheatsheaf, 1991, p. 63.

36 *The Times*, 25 July 1866, cited in Smith, *Policing Victorian London*, p. 166.

37 *The Times*, 14 November 1887. See D. C. Richter, *Riotous Victorians*, Athens, Ohio, Ohio University Press, 1981; and R. Vogler, *Reading the Riot Act*, Buckingham, Open University Press, 1991. The propertied classes of London in 1886 were incensed by the inertia of the Metropolitan Police. V. Bailey, 'The Metropolitan Police, the Home Office and the threat of outcast London', in V. Bailey, ed., *Policing and Punishment in the Nineteenth Century*, London, Croom Helm, 1981.

38 Cited in Reith, *New Study*, p. 139.

39 M. J. D. Roberts, 'Public and private in early-nineteenth century London: the Vagrant Act of 1822 and its enforcement', *Social History*, 21, 1988, p. 293.

40 S. Petrow, *Policing Morals: The Metropolitan Police and the Home Office, 1870–1914*, Oxford, Oxford University Press, 1994, *passim*. For the details of legislation see p. 294, footnote 2.

41 H. Cunningham, 'The metropolitan fairs: a case study in the control of leisure', in A. Donajgrodski, ed., *Social Control in Nineteenth Century Britain*, London, Croom Helm, 1977.

42 *Ibid.*, pp. 168–9.

43 *Ibid.*, p. 174.

44 Petrow, *Policing Morals*, p. 121. The Contagious Diseases Acts applied to eighteen garrison towns and ports and were enforced by the Metropolitan Police. Many members of the Met were unenthusiastic about the enforcement of anti-prostitution measures in London. Even a deeply religious man like Charles Warren showed an operational tolerance of prostitution that was at odds with his personal condemnation of it.

45 R. D. Storch, 'Police control of street prostitution in Victorian London', in D. Bayley, ed., *Police and Society*, London, Sage, 1977.

46 Elizabeth Cass, a dressmaker, was arrested and charged with soliciting. The case was dismissed when her employer vouched for her respectability. The action of the police and the attitude of the magistrate at Marlborough Street Police Court seemed to confirm the popular suspicion that the police indiscriminately arrested even respectable women. The d'Angely case was very similar. Madame Eva d'Angely, a Frenchwoman arrested for 'riotous and indecent behaviour', was widely seen as a respectable woman hounded by vindictive policemen and the case against her was dismissed. Again, the comments of the magistrate, suggesting that any woman walking unescorted in Regent Street was soliciting, created controversy. Petrow, *Policing Morals*, pp. 133–4, 139.

47 Nonetheless, the police could and did act with some success (and no hostility) where they had the support of popular opinion.

48 Petrow, *Policing Morals*, p. 236.

49 Successful prosecutions under the 1867 Metropolitan Streets Act were very difficult to obtain and the class-biased 1906 Street Betting Act was quickly recognised to be unenforceable by the police. *Ibid.*, chapter 10.

50 *Ibid.*, p. 297.

51 *Ibid.*, chapter 3.

52 H. Mayhew, *London Labour and London Poor*, ed. V. Neuberg, London, Penguin, 1985, pp. 15, 23, 28; P. Quennell, ed., *Mayhew's London*, London, Spring Books, 1969, p. 56.

53 Storch, 'Domestic missionary', pp. 504–5.

54 The interpretation of these figures is not straightforward. There was a general decline in the number of crimes of violence and the police may well have been fortuitous beneficiaries of this trend. However, it is possible that the police, faced with sceptical magistrates prepared to throw out poorly supported charges, became less willing to bring charges of assault against themselves. It might also be the case that there was an unwillingness to bring a charge of assault because this cast doubt on the manliness of the officer concerned. Finally, it could also be the case that the fall in the number of assaults on police officers was genuine but reflected an awareness of the power of the police and a begrudging acceptance of the fact that they were here to stay, rather than any positive acceptance of the police.

55 W. J. Fishman, *East End 1888*, London, Duckworth, 1988, p. 192.

56 P. Cohen, 'Policing the working-class city', in Bob Fine, *et al.*, eds, *Capitalism and the Rule of Law*, London, Hutchinson, 1979; and J. White, *The Worst Street in North London: Campbell Bunk, Islington Between the Wars*, London, Routledge and Kegan Paul, 1986; S. Humphries, *Hooligans or Rebels? An Oral History of Working-Class Childhood and Youth 1889–1939*, Oxford, Blackwell, 1981, p. 205.

57 V. A. C. Gattrell, 'Crime, authority and the policeman-state', in F. M. L. Thompson, ed., *Cambridge Social History*, vol. 3, Cambridge, Cambridge University Press, 1990, p. 276.

58 Cited in Storch, 'Plague', p. 80.

59 Storch, 'Plague', pp. 76–83; Bob Dobson, *Policing in Lancashire, 1839–1989*, Staining, Landy, 1989, p. 24.

60 Storch, 'Plague', pp. 76–8. Cited in Dobson, *Policing in Lancashire*, p. 26.

61 S. H. Palmer, *Police and Protest in England and Ireland, 1780–1850*, Cambridge, Cambridge University Press, 1988, rightly makes the point that in Ireland during the early 1840s there were some sixty major anti-police riots and at least sixteen fatalities, the majority of whom were peasants.

62 Storch, 'Plague', pp. 74–5.

63 A. A. Clarke, *The Policemen of Hull*, Beverley, Hutton Press, 1992, pp. 56–7, 75.

64 Robert Roberts, *The Classic Slum: Salford Life in the First Quarter of the Century*, London, Penguin, 1971, pp. 99–100; Superintendent J. Bent, *Criminal Life: Reminiscences of Forty-two Years as a Police Officer*, London, Heywood, 1891, chapter xx; T. Smethurst, *Reminiscences of a Bolton and Stalybridge Policeman, 1888–1922*, Manchester, 1983, pp. 10–12, 16–17.

65 D. Woods, 'Community violence', in J. Benson, ed., *The Working Class in England, 1875–1914*, London, Croom Helm, 1985, p. 182.

66 *Middlesbrough Weekly News*, 6 January 1865. Other incidents are taken from the watch committee reports included in the printed Council minutes, Middlesbrough. Evidence of Tom Bainbridge, interviewed December 1988.

67 B. Weinberger, 'The police and the public in mid-nineteenth century Warwickshire', in V. Bailey, ed., *Policing and Punishment in the Nineteenth Century*, London, Croom Helm, 1981.

68 R. Cowley, *Policing Northamptonshire, 1836–1986*, Studley, Brewin Books, 1986, pp. 161–8.

69 Swift, *Police Reform*, p. 36; A. Cookes, *The Southampton Police Force, 1836–1856*, Southampton, Southampton Papers, no. 8, 1972, p. 27; J. Field, 'Police, power and community in a provincial English town: Portsmouth, 1815–1875', in V. Bailey, ed., *Policing and Punishment in the Nineteenth Century*, London, Croom Helm, 1981, p. 47.

70 D. J. Elliot, *Policing Shropshire, 1836–1967*, Studley, Brewin Books, 1984, pp. 26–7; H. Hopkins, *The Long Affray: The Poaching Wars in Britain*, London, Macmillan, 1986, p. 239. A police inspector and a constable were shot by two poachers, who subsequently hanged in Reading, p. 267.

71 Hann, *Policing Victorian Dorset*, pp. 31, 43–4, 50, 54, 107; Davey, *Lawless and Immoral*; C. Emsley, 'The Bedfordshire Police, 1840–1856: a case study in the working of the Rural Constabulary Act', *Midland History*, 7, 1982. *Essex Weekly News*, 9 November 1888, cited in M. Scollan, *Sworn to Serve: Police in Essex*, Chichester, Phillimore, 1993, p. 43. See also J. Woodgate, *The Essex Police*, Lavenham, Dalton, 1983, especially photograph, p. 69.

72 D. Philips, 'Riots and public order in the Black Country 1835–60', in S. Stevenson and R. Quinault, eds, *Popular Protest and Public Order*, London, Allen & Unwin, 1974, p. 167.

73 This is the conclusion of D. Foster, 'The East Riding constabulary in the nineteenth century', *Northern History*, 21, 1985, and a similar point is made by Weinberger, 'Warwickshire', when discussing public attitudes towards the police in Birmingham. The point has a certain plausibility but by its very nature non-co-operation leaves little tangible evidence.

74 Philips, 'Riots and public order in the Black Country', p. 167; J. K. Walton and R. Poole, 'The Lancashire wakes in the nineteenth century', in R. D. Storch, ed., *Popular Culture and Custom in Nineteenth Century England*, London, Croom Helm, 1982, pp. 114–15; H. Cunningham, *Leisure in the Industrial Revolution*, London, Croom Helm, 1980, p. 24.

75 R. Malcolmson, *Popular Recreation in English Society, 1700–1850*, Cambridge, Cambridge University Press, 1981, pp. 126–36.

76 Storch, 'Please to remember', stresses the element of popular protest and notions of popular justice. This is challenged by D. G. Paz, 'Bonfire night in mid-Victorian Northants: the politics of a popular revel', *Historical Research*, 63, 1990.

77 Cited in Bob Bushway, *By Rite: Custom, Ceremony and Community in England, 1700–1870*, London, Junction Books, 1982, pp. 251–2. The advent of newer forms of football did not mean an end to trouble. 'Rough' resistance re-created itself in the form of the late-Victorian football hooligan. See E. Dunning, *et al.*, eds, *The Roots of Football Hooliganism: An Historical and Sociological Study*, London, Routledge and Kegan Paul, 1988, chapters 2–4.

78 J. Binns, *From Village to Town*, Batley, 1882, p. 139.

79 See the contemporary criticisms of C. Edwardes, 'The new football mania', *Nineteenth Century*, 37, 1892; E. Ensor, 'The football madness', *Contemporary Review*, 64, 1898; and H. F. Abell, 'The football fever', *Macmillan Magazine*, 89, 1903.

80 Middlesbrough Improvement Act 1841, 4 and 5 Victoria, cap. lxviii, para. clx, CB/M/P 58, Cleveland County Archive; Storch, 'Domestic missionary', p. 483.

81 Dobson, *Policing Lancashire*, pp. 28, 31; R. Jervis, *Chronicles of a Victorian Detective*, first published 1907, reprinted Runcorn, P. and D. Riley, 1995, p. 60.

82 J. E. King, '"We could eat the police!": popular violence in the north

Lancashire cotton strike of 1878', *Victorian Studies*, 28, 1985. Dobson, *Policing Lancashire*, p. 41.

83 D. J. V. Jones, *The Last Rising: The Newport Insurrection of 1839*, Oxford, Oxford University Press, 1985, especially pp. 224–5; J. Morgan, *Conflict and Order: The Police and Labour Disputes in England and Wales, 1900– 1939*, Oxford, Oxford University Press, 1987; and B. Weinberger, *Keeping the Peace? Policing Strikes in Britain, 1906–1926*, Oxford, Berg, 1991.

84 Roberts, *Classic Slum*, pp. 94, 99.

85 Cited in Emsley, *English Police*, p. 66.

86 D. Fitzgerald, 'A curious middle place: the Irish in Britain, 1871– 1921', in R. Swift and S. Gilley, eds, *The Irish in Britain, 1815–1939*, London, Pinter, 1989, p. 26; R. Swift, 'Crime and the Irish in nineteenth-century Britain', in R. Swift and S. Gilley, eds, *The Irish in Britain, 1815–1939*, London, Pinter, 1989, pp. 169 and 177; Davis, 'Rookeries'; and G. Davis, *The Irish in Britain, 1815–1914*, Dublin, Gill & Macmillan, 1991, especially p. 67. The quotation is from the Report of the Constabulary Commission, 1839, p. 88, para. 97, cited in Swift, 'Crime and the Irish', p. 170; Philips, 'Black Country', pp. 172–3.

87 Borough of Middlesbrough, minutes of the watch, Police and Lighting Committee, 8 October 1864, BB/M/C 2/101. The phrase in parentheses was used elsewhere by Saggerson. *Middlesbrough Weekly News*, 6 January 1865.

88 *Middlesbrough Weekly News*, 5 July 1865, 12 November 1869, and 8 December 1875.

89 Butcher, *Movable, Rambling Police*, p. 62.

90 S. Reynolds and B. and T. Woolley, *Seems So! A Working-Class View of Politics*, London, Macmillan, 1911, p. 86. Stephen Reynolds came from Devizes, Wiltshire, and studied chemistry at Manchester University. Failing to make his way as a writer in Paris, he moved to Devon. His knowledge of Sidmouth was the basis of his *A Poor Man's House*, 1909. The Woolleys were fishermen friends with whom he collaborated in his 'bottom up' view of society and politics.

91 *Ibid.*, pp. 86–7.

92 F. Thompson, *Lark Rise to Candleford*, London, Penguin, 1973, p. 484; F. M. L. Thompson, *The Rise of Respectable Society*, London, Penguin, 1988, p. 330.

93 C. T. Clarkson and J. H. Richardson, *Police!*, London, Leadenhall Press, 1888, p. 149.

94 J. Davis, 'A poor man's system of justice: the London police courts in the second half of the nineteenth century', *Historical Studies*, 27, 1984.

95 For an example of a memorial card summing up such feeling see M. Dixon, *Constabulary Duties*, Market Drayton, SB Publications, 1990, p. 84.

96 F. M. L. Thompson, 'Social control in Victorian Britain', *Economic*

History Review, 2nd series, 33, 1981; G. Stedman Jones, *Languages of Class*, Cambridge, Cambridge University Press, 1983.

97 The complex relationships that could develop with the police are well illustrated by Arthur Harding's account of his early life as a petty criminal in London, in R. Samuel, *East End Underworld: Chapters in the Life of Arthur Harding*, London, Routledge and Kegan Paul, 1981, especially chapter 15.

5

Conclusions: myth and reality

At no time were either officers or men in the force, taken as a whole, other than hard-working, honourable public servants, striving in the teeth of difficulties and dangers and hard usages of which the public knows next to nothing ... to be and to do all that they could to prevent crime, to ensure that the peace was kept and to make London a place where decent law-abiding citizens poor as well as rich, could live without fear of theft or violence. (*The Times*, 28 December 1908)

The 'bobby', archetypally in the metropolis, that avuncular figure viewed with affection and good humour by members of a grateful society, is a pervasive element of English culture. Rarely at centre stage in his own right, he is a constant and reassuring background figure, watching while others go about their daily lives. His role is encapsulated in the many photographs of late-Victorian London which show a solid, trustworthy figure, literally conducting the traffic in town, metaphorically ensuring the smooth running of society in a more general sense. So omnipresent has been the 'bobby' in popular thinking that it is easy to assume that there is something inevitable and unproblematic about his existence, and it is easy to adopt an uncritical approach to an apparently necessary and unquestionably positive force for good. The triumph of what might be called the myth of George Dixon[1] is that, for so long, the policeman was taken for granted.

However, as the preceding chapters have sought to demonstrate, the historical reality was more complex and contentious. The evolution of the new police was far from straightforward. The process of legislative change was long and often bitterly contested. Resistance to the idea of a police force was powerful and effective in the first quarter of the nineteenth century and even when the principle won more general support there was considerable debate and experimentation surrounding the precise form and nature of the new police. The structure of policing that finally came into being was a product of compromise, comprising three distinct systems and philosophies which applied to the Metropolitan Police, the borough forces and the county forces.

Turning legislative theory into practice was equally problematic. Creating an effective body of men in the counties and boroughs of England took many years. Being a policeman was no easy task. The job was always physically demanding, often dangerous. The lifestyle expected of a constable, not to mention his family, required a considerable degree of self-control and denial that set him apart and isolated him from much of the community in which he lived and worked. Often viewed as unproductive, the constable's daily routine brought him into contact and conflict not just with outright criminals (insofar as they existed) but also with ordinary men and women, who found parts of their working and leisure lives had been criminalised. There were certain advantages in being a policeman but the rewards of the job did not appear that great when set against the demands.

Undoubtedly matters changed over time. The harshness of police work was somewhat ameliorated, levels of pay improved, and the status of policing also rose. However, the emergence of the 'career' policeman, without whom a stable force could not have been created, was no short and painless process. For senior officers the frustrations and disappointments were great as men came and went, failing to make the grade. Even greater were the trials and tribulations of the ordinary constables. While the police histories contain numerous stories of the leadership triumphs in town and country, the real, but unsung, heroes were the ordinary constables who accepted the discipline asked of them, developed an ethos and *esprit de corps* of their own and made a reality, albeit less than perfect, of the aspirations of their superiors.

Finally, the creation of police legitimacy was a protracted and painful process. Policing by consent (however begrudging in certain quarters) had become a reality by the late nineteenth century. In part this was due to wider social changes which created the context in which policing took place. The gradual but continuing incorporation of the working classes into the political life of the nation, the diffusion of ideas of respectability, improvements in working-class living standards and a decline in interpersonal violence were all part of this changing context. At the same time, the police made their contribution. A belief in the principles of policing by consent and the use of minimal force combined with more pragmatic operational considerations to create a working relationship between police and policed. Discretion, the willingness to turn a blind eye, was central. Despite the fact that the balance of power shifted more in favour of the state and its agencies in the late nineteenth century, there was a limit to police power. In theory, the police controlled the civilian population but, in practice, the policed could determine the extent of that control and, in certain circumstances, impose limits on the actions of the agents of control.

By the early twentieth century the police were an established fact of life. Positively welcomed by the overwhelming majority of the middle and upper classes, they also had considerable working-class support. However, such support was often given begrudgingly and deep-rooted hostilities, dating back to the earliest days of the new police and reinforced by subsequent experiences, were to be found near to the surface. Violence towards the police remained an everyday matter and, at times of particular tension, popular hostility assumed serious proportions. In a society still much divided in both material and moral terms, it was difficult to escape the conclusion that police and policed were on different sides. As one Edwardian working-class commentator observed:

> the police is the means they've a-got for forcing their ways an' their convenience on the likes o' us. That's what the police is; an so long they'm that, 'twon't be no better; 'cause although the police belongs rightly to the likes of us, 'tis bound to be to the police's advantage for to play up to the likes o' they.[2]

Notes

1   George Dixon was the fictional London bobby who first appeared in the 1950 film *The Blue Lamp*. In the film he was shot after twenty minutes,

but he was brought back to life in 1956 for the BBC television series *Dixon of Dock Green*. Dixon, played by Jack Warner, became the embodiment of the comforting, avuncular community policeman. Although this figure was already out of date in the 1950s, this has not prevented people in the 1990s demanding a return to such policing.

2   S. Reynolds and B. and T. Woolley, *Seems So! A Working-Class View of Politics*, London, Macmillan, 1911, p. 95.

Selected documents

Section 1. General interpretations

Document 1

An early-twentieth-century police historian states his view of the police as public servants. Captain W. L. Melville Lee, 'Co-operative police and the suppression of riots', *A History of Police in England*, London, Methuen, 1901, chapter xvi, pp. 328–9.

The members of the English police are public servants in the fullest sense of the term; not servants of any individual, of any particular class or sect, but servants of the whole community – excepting only that part of it which in setting the law at defiance, has thereby become a public enemy. The strength of the Man in Blue, properly understood, lies in the fact that he has behind him the whole weight of public opinion; for he only wages war against the law-breaker, and in this contest he can claim the goodwill of every loyal citizen.... The basis upon which our theory of police ultimately rests, is the assumption that every lawful act performed by a police officer in the execution of his duty, has the sanction and approval of the great majority of his fellow-citizens; and under our constitution it would be impossible for any constabulary force to continue in existence, if its actions persistently ran counter to the expressed wishes of the people....

Year by year, in spite of occasional setbacks, the English police have risen in the estimation of their fellow-countrymen until they have won for themselves a position in the minds of the people which for respect and regard is without a parallel in Europe.

Document 2

The orthodox view of the new police as a response to the collapse of law and order. Charles Reith, *A Short History of the British Police*, Oxford, Oxford University of Press, 1948, pp. 3–4, 44, 109.

The almost complete impotence of law-enforcement machinery in England during the later years of the eighteenth and the early years of the nineteenth centuries was rightly regarded as a serious menace to state existence. A new form of police had not only to be found; it had to be invented, because the only other model which was in existence in the world was feared and hated by the people of England to an extent which led many of them to believe, sincerely, that what they would be obliged to endure from it, if it were adopted in England, would be worse than what they were suffering from lack of police. These sufferings increased until they became intolerable and led, at last, to the provision and establishment of the existing third system of police. The 'New Police' as they were called, quickly ended a long period of uncontrollable crime and disorder which had lasted, in some parts of the country, for more than a century....

Rarely in the history of Britain have certain unique underlying qualities of the character of her people been so clearly illustrated as they were by the men of the New Police.... These details enhance the wonder of the miracle of what the New Police achieved in the first years of their existence, and of their triumphs over their incredible sufferings....

The basic secret of the success and efficiency of the British police is not far to seek. It lies almost wholly, in the unique relationship with the public which the police have created and are at constant pains to maintain. It has been noted ... that the achievement of this relationship as it exists today was deliberately planned by the early leaders of the police at a time when public hatred of them almost stultified their efforts to do their duty.

Document 3

The revisionist view of the new police as agents of social control. R. D. Storch, 'The plague of blue locusts: police reform and popular resistance in northern England, 1840–57', *International Review of Social History*, 20, 1975, pp. 61, 62, 64.

The implantation of a modern police in the industrial districts of Northern England resulted from a new consensus among the propertied classes that it was necessary to create a professional, bureaucratically organized lever of urban discipline and permanently introduce it into the heart of working-class communities. The coming of the new police represented a significant extension into hitherto geographically peripheral areas of both the moral and political authority of the state. This was to be accomplished by the creation of a powerful and quite modern device – a bureaucracy of official morality....

The mission of the new police was a symptom of both a profound social change and a deep rupture in class relations in the first half of the nineteenth century. By this time, both the actions and the 'language' spoken by the urban masses were, if intelligible at all, deeply frightening....

For these reasons the police received an omnibus mandate: to detect and prevent crime; to maintain a constant, unceasing pressure of surveillance upon all facets of life in working-class communities – to report on political opinion and movements, trade-union activities, public house and recreational life.

Document 4

The new police presented as moral missionaries. R. D. Storch, 'The policeman as domestic missionary', *Social History*, 9, 1976, pp. 481, 496.

Historians of the police, public order, and the criminal law have understandably concentrated on the role of the police in the repression of crime, public disorder and popular political movements or have studied the police from the point of view of social administration. The police had a broader mission in the nineteenth century, however – to act as an all-purpose lever of urban discipline. The imposition of the police brought the arm of municipal and state authority directly to bear upon the institutions of daily life in working-class neighbourhoods, touching off a running battle with local custom and popular culture which lasted at least until the end of the century.... In northern industrial towns of England these police functions must be viewed as a direct complement to the attempts of urban middle-class elites – by means of sabbath, educational, temperance and recreational reform – to mold a laboring class amenable to new disciplines of both work and leisure. The other side of the coin of middle-class voluntaristic moral and social reform (even when sheathed) was the policeman's truncheon....

The police ... once successfully installed confronted a number of serious problems in the discharge of their moral-reform mission. Many problems proved utterly intractable, leading some police authorities to quickly gauge the real limits of their effectiveness in these areas. Though the full measure of change could never be fully lived up to, the nineteenth century saw the forging of a modern and generally effective technique of order-keeping: the installation of the eyes and ears of ruling elites in the very centres of working-class life.

Document 5

A recent assessment of the orthodox and revisionist interpretations. R. Reiner, *The Politics of the Police*, 2nd edn, Hemel Hempstead, Harvester Wheatsheaf, 1992, pp. 55–6.

All historians of the emergence of professional policing in Britain have shown that it was surrounded by acute political conflict. The orthodox historians are clearly wrong in their lack of appreciation of the rational basis of opposition to the police, rooted in different social interests and political philosophies. On the other hand, the revisionists over-emphasise the extent of continued working-class opposition, and the overt role of the police in class and political control. While not securing the quick and relatively painless passage into acceptance suggested by the Reithians, the police did gain increasing acquiescence from substantial sections of the working class, not only as the result of 'soft' service activities, but in their 'hard' law enforcement and order maintenance function. The police succeeded in acquiring this degree of legitimacy, in which they were no longer seen as a politically oppressive force, by a combination of specific strategies which gave the British police a unique character. I would claim that a *neo-Reithian* framework is the most appropriate for understanding this. This is a perspective which would give due weight to the success of the police reformers and the tradition they created, but also recognises that policing is embedded in a social order riven by structured bases of conflict, not fundamental integration.

Section 2. *The introduction of the new police*

Document 6

An analysis of the problem of order in the early nineteenth century. P. Colquhoun, *A Treatise on the Police of the Metropolis*, London, Bye & Law, 1806, pp. 24–5.

From what has been thus stated, is it not fair to conclude, that the want of security which the Public experiences with regard to life and property, and the inefficacy of the Police in preventing crimes, are to be attributed principally to the following causes?

1. The imperfections in the Criminal Code; and in many instances, its deficiency with respect to the mode of punishment: as well as to the want of many other regulations, provisions and restraints, applicable to the present state of Society for the purpose of preventing crimes.

2. The want of an active principle, calculated to concentrate and connect the whole Police of the Metropolis and the Nation; and to reduce the general management to a system and method, by the interposition of a superintending agency, composed of able, intelligent and indefatigable men, acting under the direction and control of His Majesty's Principal Secretary of State for the Home Department.

Document 7

The 1818 Select Committee's reasons for not recommending change. Third Report of the Select Committee on the Police of the Metropolis, *Parliamentary Papers*, 1818 (423), viii, pp. 32–3.

The police of a free country is to be found in rational and humane laws, in an effective and enlightened magistracy, and in the judicious and proper selection of those officers of justice in whose hands, as conservators of the people, executive duties are legally placed; but above all, on the moral habits and opinions of the people; and in proportion as these approximate towards a state of perfection, so that people may rest in security; and though their property may occasionally be invaded, or their lives endangered by the hands of wicked and desperate individuals, yet the institutions of the country being sound, its laws well administered, and justice executed against offenders, no greater safeguard can be obtained, without sacrificing all those rights which society was instituted to preserve.

Document 8

The continuing fear of the police as a threat to liberty prevents reform. Select Committee on the Police of the Metropolis, *Parliamentary Papers*, 1822 (440), iv, p. 11.

It is difficult to reconcile an effective system of police with the perfect freedom of action and exemption from interference, which are the real privileges and blessings of society in this country; and your Committee think that the forfeiture or curtailment of such advantages would be too great a sacrifice for improvement in police, or facilities in detection of crime, however desirable in themselves if abstractedly considered.

Document 9

Concern with the unreformed police in the late 1820s. J. Hardwick, 'Police', *Quarterly Review*, 37, 1828, pp. 502, 504.

For upward of two centuries has police [*sic*] continued nearly in the same deteriorated and imbecile condition, with scarcely a single effort on the part of the legislature, either to revive and adapt old institutions, or devise new ones, more, perhaps, in unison with the present state of society; and this, although every neighbouring country around us has its ameliorated code of police and criminal procedure. Statute, it is true, has been heaped upon statute: but each passed on the spur of the occasion, without regard to principle or system.... If police was at any time their object, it was rather that of parks and poachers, than protection of persons; not so much to keep down felons, as to keep up pheasants; and that it might not lose its character for consistency, in always being most defective, when and where most wanted – the metropolitan county came to be dis-tinguished above all the rest, for the incompetence and venality of its justices.... It is absolutely necessary to incorporate the present discordant, coarse, and corrupt elements, called, or miscalled watchmen, patroles, petty constables, headboroughs, streetkeepers, &c. &c., into one vigorous and well-organized whole – a regular police force – characterized in its movements by activity and unity, its members by respectability, and its superintendence by unceasing vigilance: this body, too, should be placed exclusively under the control of a ministerial, not a judicial officer, of suitable consideration, nominated by the Home Secretary, and independent of all other interference.

In limine there can be no doubt that the whole of the existing watch-system of London and its vicinity ought to be mercilessly struck to the ground. No human being has even the slightest confidence in it. Scenes of collusion, tricks, compromises, knaveries of all kinds, are brought to light daily: none of the magistrates rest the least faith on the statements of these functionaries, unless when they are backed by the testimonies of other persons. The feelings against them is strong, exactly in proportion as opportunity of learning their real habits has been abundant. Their existence is a nuisance and a curse; and are they to be upheld, in order that vestrymen may provide for worthless or worn-out dependants, at the expense of the peace and security of such population and such property?

Document 10

Changing opinions in the late 1820s. Critics of the old system of policing give evidence. Report of the Select Committee on the Police of the Metropolis, *Parliamentary Papers*, 1828, (533), vi, pp. 175, 257, 269.

H M Dyer Esq., magistrate of the Marlborough-street police office: Respectable tradesmen, from a feeling of duty, are sometimes induced to act as constables in their own right, but when they do so, it is deplorable to see how awkwardly they bear their unwonted burden. They commonly know nothing of their duty when they commence, and they are only just beginning to learn it when their turn of annual service has nearly expired. But generally speaking ... respectable tradesmen will not be found to undertake so onerous an office, and thus it passes into the hands of substitutes, who although they may learn their business by longer apprenticeship to it, are too often wanting in respectability, and chargeable with great misconduct. The remedy for this evil in metropolitan parishes would be, to make the constables permanent officers, with fixed and respectable remuneration for their services.

A B Richmond, St. Luke's parish: Most of [our watchmen] do [have other occupations]; we have selected as many pensioners as we could obtain; the character of the watchmen is better, as to moral and physical powers; we take none under five feet seven inches in height, and we always have a character produced.... We could not obtain men of good moral character and physical powers from our own parish; out of about ninety-two that we required, we only got eight or ten parishioners that answered our description.

Mr. Edward Edmonds, Reporter to the *Morning Chronicle*: But the numerous robberies that have been committed lately appeared to me to be owing to the defective state of the night police: it applies chiefly to the watch, knowing they are so ill paid, and many of them bad characters indeed, who for half a crown, in my opinion, might be bribed to let a prisoner go, or take a prisoner. I have seen some of the worst characters, when they have been discharged by a magistrate at one parish, put on at another parish. I have known that in an instance which I witnessed in Bow-street, opposite the office, in which [*sic*] the man died in consequence of the injury which he sustained: I complained to the Board of Covent-garden parish; he was removed, but afterwards put upon the watch in another parish; he was notoriously in the pay of the brothels in the neighbourhood, to suffer the girls to go about the streets to pick up men; and many of the watchmen are in the pay of those persons.

Document 11

The recommendation of the 1828 Select Committee. Report of the Select Committee on the Police of the Metropolis, *Parliamentary Papers*, 1828 (533), vi, pp. 30–1.

Your Committee trust that they have now established, as they proposed to establish, from authority of previous Committees, and from Evidence to recent facts, that there is a strong presumption in favour of a material change in the system of Police which at present exists in the Metropolis and its neighbourhood.... [T]hey are strongly inclined to recommend a Plan, of which the following Suggestions contain the general outline:

THAT there should be constituted an Office of Police acting under the immediate directions of the Secretary of State for the Home Department, upon which should be devolved the general control over the whole of the Establishments of Police of every denomination, including the Nightly Watch:

THAT the immediate superintendence of this department should extend over a circumference comprizing the whole of that thickly inhabited district which may be considered to include the Metropolis and its environs:

THAT the Magistrates attached to this office, should be relieved from the discharge of those ordinary duties which necessarily occupy so much of the time of the present Police Magistrates; and that they should be the centre of an intimate and constant communication with the other Police Offices on all matters relating to the disturbance of the public peace, and to the commission of all offences of a serious character.

Document 12

Edwin Chadwick advocates preventive policing, 1829. E. Chadwick, 'Preventative policing', *London Review*, 1829, pp. 252, 253–5.

Our present police consist of disjointed bodies of men governed separately, under heterogeneous regulations, and acting for the most part, under the earliest set of expedients: and then only upon being called upon, seizing or receiving in charge an offender and handing him over to the judicature for punishment. A good police would be one well-organised body of men acting upon a system of precautions, to prevent crimes and public calamities; to preserve the public peace and order; and to perform whatever other useful functions might be comprehended in their duties without hindering the performance of those of the most important nature in the best manner....

If a foreign jurist were to view the present condition of the metropolis ... he would find the metropolis divided and subdivided into petty jurisdictions, each independent of each other; each having distinctly different interests to engender perpetual jealousies and animosities, and being sufficiently free from any general control to prevent any intercommunity of information, or any unity of action. He would find that information gained in one district, unless communicated by accident, is lost to all others; and that a gang of thieves whose systematic operations have excited alarm in one neighbourhood, are enabled to decamp to another, which knowing no danger, takes no precaution for its safety, and that thus the thieves are enabled to recommence operations with renewed chances of impunity. He might discover that officers, and a display of protection to the inhabitants, were requisite to the success of the thieves; for otherwise the work of prevention might ultimately be taken into their own hands; a course which, judging from several instances where it has already been adopted, would be fatal to systematic depredation.

The various officers who are appointed for the protection of property during the day, have either inadequate salaries, or no salaries whatever; and as their emoluments depend on the demand for their services in pursuing thieves and recovering stolen goods, they have a direct interest that robberies should be numerous, and that property to a considerable value should be taken, in order that large rewards may be offered for its recovery.

But the most extensive plunder is obtained during the night; and the details of the organization of the nightly watch are felicitously adapted to suit the convenience of the plunderers. The watchmen have mostly fixed stations (in boxes which accommodate them for repose) that it may be seen with certainty where they are, and that advantage may be taken of the opportunity significantly offered to carry on operations in security where they are not. But to add to this security, the rounds of the watchmen are made to take place at known and fixed intervals of sufficient length to allow the removal of considerable booty; and lest, whilst intent on their work, the thieves might permit themselves to be surprised at the expiration of the allowed time, they are warned of its expiration by the lugubrious notes which announce the watchman's distant and slow approach. That they may not inadvertently fall into his way, he is distinguished by his dress; and his lantern renders him an 'ambulating lighthouse' to direct their perilous course.

Document 13

Peel and Wellington give their reasons for reform, 1829. Speeches on the Metropolis Police Bill, House of Commons, 15 April 1829, and House of Lords, 5 June 1829. *Parliamentary Debates*, 2nd Series, 1829, cols 868, 880–1, 1750–1.

Mr. Secretary Peel: These different committees [in 1770, 1793, 1812, 1818, 1822 and 1828] had been the result of alarm at some respectable or unprecedented outrage at the time; or the effect, perhaps, of a general conviction that crimes and offences against the peace of society were so much on the increase, as to require an increased and corresponding vigour on the part of our police.... Whoever had read the reports of those committees, particularly those of late date, would find the state of our police to be most defective. It had been pretty clearly ascertained, that it was altogether unsafe, and that it had been so for a long period, to commit the care of the lives and properties of the people of the metropolis and its vicinity to the charge of the parochial watch, during the part of the twenty-four hours which constituted the object of their very lax and inefficient protection.... He was not one who considered that this increase of criminals had been mainly occasioned by the increase of distress amongst the population. He believed that these criminals were, in almost all instances, trained and hardened profligates, – that they had been incited to the commission of crime, by the temptation which the present lax system of policing held out to them; and he was sure it was possible effectually to check them, by the vigorous exercise of the powers supplied by the common law of the land....

The Duke of Wellington: ... there could be no doubt that no branch connected with the administration of public justice in this country was so defective as the police. This was clearly proved by the great increase in crime in the metropolis. It appeared from the returns, that in the last six years the total number of criminals committed for various offences had increased in the ratio of two-fifths.... It was perfectly clear to all who had considered the subject, that this rapid increase in crime arose solely from the deficiency of the police. Their lordships must know, that the state of the watch in most of the parishes of the metropolis was most inefficient. Indeed nothing could possibly be more so. And though the state of the watch was thus confessedly inefficient, yet, from events which had recently occurred, it was well ascertained that the watch was exceedingly expensive to parishes.... In the metropolis itself – in Westminster – where there was a watch in every parish, the system was so badly arranged, that there was no co-operating communication between the watchmen of one parish and those of another; and even in the same parish there were frequently different watch-establishments governed by different local authorities. In St. Pancras, there were no less than eighteen different establishments, formed under different acts of parliament, not one of them having any communication with another. The consequence was, that the watchmen of one district were content with driving thieves from their own particular neighbourhood, into that which adjoined it.

Document 14

The Whigs consider a national police force, 1832. *Observations upon the Draft of a Bill for the Establishment of an Efficient Police in such Towns and Districts in England and Wales as May Require the Same.* Cited by D. Philips and R. D. Storch, 'Whigs and coppers: the Grey ministry's national police scheme, 1832', *Historical Research*, 67, 1994, pp. 87–90.

A discretionary power may be given to the government, to establish a constabulary force, on the model of the Metropolitan Police, under such limitations and regulations as may appear to be convenient.... [T]his principle is that upon which the accompanying draft of a bill has been framed, and seems to be the only one which can be adopted with prudence, and at the same time with any chance of a favourable result. It is impossible to be insensible, that it demands for the government a large power; but it is not so large as it seems. The success of such a measure would depend entirely upon the discretion, the prudence, the temper, the caution, with which it was carried into execution; and no government would attempt to enforce an increased police establishment upon any city or district, without having first ascertained that it was necessary, and that it was desired by the more respectable and intelligent portion of the inhabitants. The Metropolitan Police was imposed by law, but it was not imposed until the necessity of it had been established before more than one committee of the house of commons, not until it was certain that it would meet with the general approbation of those, for whose advantage and security it was intended. This bill will give the government the power of feeling the pulse of the people, of discovering the parts of the country in which a stronger power of police is both wanted and wished for, of taking advantage of this disposition, where it exists, of consulting the public feeling upon the subject, and of thus introducing a better administration of justice and a more effectual enforcement of law, throughout the whole of the community.

Document 15

The 1839 Select Committee argues for the creation of an efficient rural police. First Report of the Commissioners appointed to inquire as to the best means of establishing an efficient Constabulary Force in the Counties of England and Wales, *Parliamentary Papers*, 1839 (169), xix, pp. 99, 103, 137, 184.

We find that the primary function of 'watch and ward' which form a necessary incident of the duties of the constabulary have entirely fallen into desuetude, which is ascribable to the dereliction of the constitutional principle of local responsibility to the supreme executive for the prevention of crime. As a consequence of this state of things we find private watchmen extensively employed by individuals and by associations for self-protection....

Three of the constables of this parish [Speen, Newbury] are reputedly drunkards, and one is the brother of a beer-house keeper, whose house is notoriously disorderly ... rural parochial constables [around Lincoln] are generally very ignorant men, and useless for the purpose of police; all kinds of evil necessarily arise out of this state of things....

Before the introduction of the police, brought down from London about three or perhaps four years ago, not only was the town itself exposed to constant disturbance and depredations, but farmers in the neighbouring villages were often robbed of their poultry, sheep and other farm produce.... [T]here is not a better regulated town anywhere now than this parish of Wymondham. The vigilance of the police makes the introduction of stolen property into the town so difficult and so hazardous that thieving is nothing like so good a trade as it used to be; and yet there are but three officers, who keep the population in order, and scour a tract of 10,000 acres, terrifying the thieves out of their occupation....

Not a single burglary has been committed in the borough [of Hull] since the establishment of the new police ... there are no street robberies; serious crimes have greatly diminished; violent and brutal assaults, especially on females, have been of frequent occurrence, but none have taken place since the formation of the force....

We therefore propose

I THAT AS A PRIMARY REMEDY FOR THE EVILS SET FORTH, A PAID CONSTABULARY FORCE SHOULD BE TRAINED, APPOINTED AND ORGANIZED ON THE PRINCIPLES OF MANAGEMENT, RECOGNISED BY THE LEGISLATURE IN THE APPOINTMENT OF THE NEW METROPOLITAN POLICE....

IV THAT THE CONSTABLES SO APPOINTED SHALL REPORT THEIR PROCEEDINGS TO THE MAGISTRATES OF THE QUARTER AND PETTY SESSIONS WHERE THEY ARE SITUATED....

VII THAT THE COMMISSIONERS SHALL FRAME RULES AND REGULATIONS FOR THE GENERAL MANAGEMENT OF THE POLICE, WHICH RULES SHALL, ON THE APPROBATION OF THE SECRETARY OF STATE, BE BINDING.

Document 16

A Select Committee argues for greater uniformity, 1853. Second Report of the Select Committee on Police, *Parliamentary Papers*, 1853 (715), xxxvi, pp. iii–iv.

The Select Committee appointed to consider the expediency of adopting a more Uniform System of Police in England and Wales ... have agreed to report the following RESOLUTIONS....

Resolved, 1. That the Act ... commonly called the Rural Police Act, has (from the permissive character of its enactments), failed to provide such a general and uniform Constabulary Force as, in the opinion of Your Committee, is essentially required for the prevention of crime and security of property.

Resolved, 2. That in the districts in which the Rural Police Act has been adopted, its efficiency for the prevention of crime, by rendering the detection and apprehension of offenders more prompt and certain, has been proved to the satisfaction of Your Committee; that it has tended to the maintenance of order, and the improved habits of the population; that vagrancy has greatly decreased and, more especially in combination with the casual relief order of the Poor Law Board, has been, in some places, almost entirely suppressed; and the effectual protection afforded to property peculiarly exposed to depredation, has, in the opinion of owners and holders of land, rendered its occupation more desirable. The adoption of the Rural Police, therefore, in the opinion of Your Committee, has proved highly advantageous to those districts, whether tested by moral, social, or economical considerations.

Resolved, 3. That the Superintending Constables appointed under the 5th & 6th Vict. c.109, have proved useful as Police officers, to the extent of their individual exertions and services within their respective divisions, but that the appointment of a Superintending Constable in each petty sessional division provides no remedy for the inefficiency of the Parochial Constables; and it is the opinion of Your Committee that any system of Police mainly dependent on the aid of Parochial Constables, must prove ineffectual for the protection of property, more especially that of the poorer classes, for the prompt detection and pursuit of offenders, the maintenance of order, and other duties of a Police Force, for which their necessary avocations and local connexions entirely disqualify them....

Resolved, 6. That the efficiency of all existing Police Forces is materially impaired by the want of co-operation between the Rural Constabulary and the Police under the control of the authorities of the boroughs, or other local jurisdictions. That, in order to secure that co-operation which uniformity alone can afford, Your Committee are of opinion, that the smaller boroughs should be consolidated with districts or counties for Police purposes, and that the Police in the larger boroughs should be under a similar system of management and control to that of the adjoining district or county and (where practicable) under the same superintendence, by which arrangement a considerable saving would be effected in the general expenditure....

Resolved, 8. That it is the opinion of Your Committee, that it is most desirable that legislative measures should be introduced without delay by Her Majesty's Government, rendering the adoption of an efficient Police Force on a uniform principle throughout Great Britain.

Section 3. *Creating an effective force*

Document 17

Guidance given to Birmingham police, 1839. Birmingham City, Instruction Orders, 1839, Birmingham Reference Library, 64854. Cited in A. H. Manchester, *Sources of English Legal History, 1750–1950*, London, Butterworths, 1984, pp. 248–50.

But the first Duty of a Constable is always to *prevent* the commission of a crime.... A Constable may arrest one whom he has just cause to suspect to be about to commit a felony. Thus, when a drunken person, or a man in a violent passion, threatens the life of another, the Constable should interfere and arrest.

He should arrest any person having in his possession any picklock-key, crow, jack, bit or other implement with intent feloniously to break into any dwelling-house, warehouse, coach-house, stable, or out-building; or any person armed with any gun, pistol, hanger, cutlass, bludgeon or offensive weapon....

If after sunset, and before sunrising, the Constable shall see any one carrying a bundle of goods, which he suspects were stolen, he should stop and examine the person, and may detain him; but here also he should judge from the circumstances (such as the appearance and manner of the party, his account of himself and the like), whether he really has got stolen goods, before he actually takes him into custody....

In cases of actual breaches of the peace, as riots, affrays, assaults and the like, committed within the view of the Constable, he should immediately interfere (first giving public notice of his Office, if he be not already known), separate the combatants, and prevent others from joining in the affray. If the riot, &c. be of a serious nature, or if the offenders do not immediately desist, he should take them into custody, securing also the principal instigators of the tumult, and doing everything in his power to restore quiet....

The Constable ought to arrest and take before a Justice any person walking about the streets and exposing to view in the street any obscene print or exhibition, or any person, wilfully, openly and obscenely, in any street or place of public resort, exposing his person, with intent to insult any female....

When insane persons or children are found wandering in the streets, unable to give an account of their residences, they are to be taken charge of by the Police and brought to the nearest Police Station....

The Constable has power to apprehend and carry before a Justice of the Peace every common prostitute wandering in the public streets or public highways, or in any place of public resort, and behaving in a riotous or indecent manner, – Every person wandering abroad or placing himself or herself in any public street or highway, court or passage, to beg or gather alms, or causing or procuring any child to do so, all such being declared by the law to be idle and disorderly persons, – Every person wandering abroad and lodging in any barn or outhouse, or in any deserted or unoccupied building, or in the open air, or under a tent, or in any cart or waggon, not having any visible means of subsistence, and not giving a good account of himself or herself, – Every person wandering abroad and endeavouring, by the exposure of wounds or deformities, to obtain or gather alms, – Every person playing or betting in any street, road, highway, or other open or public place, at or with any table or instrument of gaming at any game, or pretended game of chance.

Document 18

Guidance for the Lancashire police. Cited in Bob Dobson, *Policing in Lancashire, 1839–1989*, Staining, Landy, 1989, p. 23.

COUNTY OF LANCASTER CONSTABULARY FORCE

THE FOLLOWING MAXIMS
Are to be strictly observed and borne in mind by the Constables of the Force

1. Constables are placed in authority to PROTECT, not to OPPRESS, the Public.

2. To do which effectually, they must earnestly and systematically exert themselves to PREVENT CRIME.

3. When a crime has been committed, no time should be lost, nor exertions spared, to discover and bring to justice the OFFENDERS.

4. Obtain a knowledge of all REPUTED THIEVES and IDLE and DISORDERLY PERSONS.

5. Watch narrowly all Persons having NO VISIBLE MEANS OF SUBSISTENCE.

6. Prevent VAGRANCY.

7. Be IMPARTIAL in the discharge of duty.

8. Discard from the mind all POLITICAL and SECTARIAN prejudices.

9. Be COOL and INTREPID in the discharge of duties in emergencies and unavoidable conflicts.

10. Avoid ALTERCATIONS, and display PERFECT COMMAND of TEMPER under INSULT and gross PROVOCATION, to which all Constables must occasionally be liable.

11. NEVER STRIKE but in SELF DEFENCE, nor treat a Prisoner with more Rigour than may be absolutely necessary to prevent escape.

12. Practice [sic] the most complete SOBRIETY, one instance of DRUNKENNESS will render a Constable liable to DISMISSAL.

13. Treat with the utmost CIVILITY all classes of HER MAJESTY'S SUBJECTS, and cheerfully render ASSISTANCE to all in need of it.

14. Exhibit DEFERENCE and RESPECT to the MAGISTRACY.

15. Promptly and cheerfully OBEY all SUPERIOR OFFICERS.

16. Render an HONEST, FAITHFUL, and SPEEDY account of all MONIES and PROPERTY, whether intrusted with them for others, or taken possession of in the execution of duty.

17. With reference to the foregoing, bear especially in mind that 'HONESTY IS THE BEST POLICY.'

18. Be perfectly neat and clean in Person and Attire.

19. Never sit down in a PUBLIC HOUSE or BEER SHOP.

20. **AVOID TIPPLING.**

21. It is the interest of every man to devote some portion of his spare time to the practice of READING and WRITING and the general improvement of his mind.

22. IGNORANCE is an insuperable bar to promotion.

J. WOODFORD
Chief Constable

Document 19

Advice to the Huntingdonshire constabulary. Chief Constable's General Memo No. 2, 28 June 1857. Cited in C. Emsley, *The English*

Selected documents

Police: A Social and Political History, Hemel Hempstead, Harvester Wheatsheaf, 1991, p. 72.

The immediate attention of the Constabulary is directed to the conducting and time keeping of public houses and Beer shops according to Law but as a preliminary every house which has not already, is to be called at and informed that such Law will be enforced and no proceedings taken where such caution has not been given neither shall I in any *first* instance sanction proceedings to be taken for less time than half an hour's default, but thereafter cases of obstinate perseverance and resistance are to be brought to my notice, in like manner furious driving. The encampments of Gypsies and others driving without reins, stoppage and obstructions by carts, wagons, etc at Public Houses in the absence of drivers within are to be put down....

Obstructions and profanations of the sabbath are to be attended to as far as the Law admits and with judicious management may be put stop to....

In this first year I wish to have no *display* whatever of Police Force at the various village feasts or meetings beyond the presence of the located P.C. (and the Superintendent himself when convenient) and no interference on his part not imperatively called for, such appearance before the people are used to it being rather calculated to induce disturbance than otherwise, but thereafter improved order will be expected from such attendance as may be directed and any extension of the restricted time of holdings prevented....

Travelling hawkers are to be looked after, their licences demanded and in the absence of any, proceedings to be taken. The itinerant 'Tape and Bobbin' and such like parties should be accompanied throughout villages and the support of the inhabitants solicited to discountenance these spies and advanced couriers of the Thieves to follow. But above all the interminable war is to be made on all 'Tramps' of every description with which this county appears to be infested to an extraordinary extent, and now that every county has its Police according to the conduct of the Constabularies towards them will they more or less determine their beats thereafter.

Document 20

Advice to constables, 1894. P. Bicknell, *The Police Manual*, 11th edn, London, 1894, pp. 10–11.

A Constable's Deportment

It may be observed that the efficiency of a Constable, in any locality, will greatly depend upon his own individual bearing and conduct. Possessing, as he will, great powers of interference with others, he will recommend himself to the respect and confidence of those amongst whom he is stationed by a conciliatory and forbearing style of deportment. To be exercising austere authority upon every little occasion that may call for his interference will be to excite the ill-feeling of all observers; whilst the exhibition of good-tempered forbearance and friendly persuasion will not only enlist their sympathies, but, in the end, will greatly assist him in fulfilling those numerous and useful duties which the law of the country has charged him to execute.

Document 21

Problems of recruitment and retainment in a rural force. Captain J. B. B. McHardy, Report of the Chief Constable to the Magistrates of the County of Essex, 15 October 1850. Reprinted as Appendix 1 to Select Committee on Police, *Parliamentary Papers*, 1853 (715), xxxvi, p. 146.

The difficulty of procuring proper men for county policemen is apparent from the qualifications required being not only high character and physical power, but also great energy and intelligence; for in consequence of the dispersed nature of the force, a county policeman is generally less under supervision and more called upon to judge and act for himself than a serjeant in the metropolitan police, who receives the same pay as an inspector in this force (viz., 25s. per week), who while exercising supervision discharges also all the duties of a private constable....

I assure you that a large proportion of the private constables are really sagacious, intrepid and valuable men, who would do credit to any establishment. Good men are tempted to join the force on the lowest class, not merely for the 17s. a week, but by the hope that by doing their duty they may rise to the 19s. and 21s., in fact to the highest offices in the force, and to secure to themselves a permanent situation and salary.

Document 22

The problems of an urban force. *Middlesbrough Weekly News*, 14 April 1865.

On the reading of the minutes of the Watch Committee, Councillor Lacy complained that so many changes were being made in the police force. It seemed to him that no sooner did an officer get to know the bad characters of the town than he left the force. He thought this was very unsatisfactory and not at all conducive to the efficiency of the force. Alderman Richardson explained that it was in consequence of the high rate of wages paid in the town and district that the men were so often leaving the force. They had increased the pay of the constables from time to time purposely to meet this difficulty.

Document 23

The work of a policeman, 1902. James Greenwood, *The Prisoner in the Dock*, London, Chatto & Windus, 1902, pp. 2–5.

His duties are not what may be called arduous, but to a man used to an active life they must – at all events until he becomes accustomed to them – be indescribably irksome. His walk on beat is a dreary dawdle, and must not exceed two miles an hour. In blazing summer-time he is not free to choose between the sunny side and the shady, and in rain, hail, or snow he must doggedly face the unkind elements.

It is, of course, much worse at night-time. By the rules of the service he is denied the solace of a pipe even in his dark and solitary perambulations, and he is even more strictly prohibited from indulging in a comforting nip from a pocket flask.... But though the authorities prohibit indulgence in alcoholic stimulant by policemen, either on day or night duty, a kindly regard is manifested for those on the beat from dark till daylight in outlying and suburban districts. Constables so engaged are privileged to carry with them coffee, ready-made in a tin bottle, and a spirit-lamp, by means of which they may enjoy a hot and nourishing drink at a time when they most require it.

The young fellow who contemplates joining the force finds but little in the idea to stimulate his ambition or his patriotism.... If he has inquired into the matter at all, he knows that, unless favoured with extraordinary luck, it is only by slow and sure painstaking and careful attention to his duties he can hope, in the course of three or four years, to qualify himself for promotion, which may bring him three or four shillings a week, and after he has seen probably some ten years' service, he is made a sergeant. Meanwhile he plods on.

Document 24

The dangers of being a policeman in London. Samuel Smiles, 'The police of London', *Quarterly Review*, 129, 1870, pp. 125–6.

The principal diseases to which they are subject, as might be expected, are of the lungs and air-passages, the results of their constant exposure to vicissitudes of temperature. Out of about 800 men who are on the sick-list monthly, from 300 to 400, during the winter months, suffer from catarrh, bronchitis, sore throat, and rheumatism; while of the 63 deaths in 1868, 27 were from consumption. But, beside these diseases of exposure, the police are exposed to risks of wounds and injuries, which tend greatly to swell the list of disabled men. Thus, in 1868, not fewer than 1130 suffered from fractures, dislocations, wounds and miscellaneous injuries in the execution of their duty, or an average of about 100 cases a month....

The greater number of the men thus wounded and disabled received their injuries while apprehending criminals, or in the attempts made by criminals to escape and of bystanders to rescue them by force. Not fewer than eighty men were disabled in this way. Forty-two were knocked down, kicked and otherwise maltreated. Eighteen were permanently injured by drunken persons; nine by riotous or disorderly roughs; seven by burglars; six by Irish mobs; five by miscellaneous mobs; five by drunken soldiers and militiamen. Six were stabbed by prisoners, one a convicted thief. Three were severely injured by falling while in the pursuit of thieves, one from a roof, another from a wall, and a third by being tripped-up to enable a thief to escape. One constable was shot by a highwayman, and another by a criminal he had brought to justice. One had his leg broken when apprehending a prisoner, another had his wrist dislocated, and a third his knee-cap. Among the remaining cases, we find several injuries by being jumped upon by ruffians, kicked by prostitutes, knocked down by runaway horses which they were trying to stop, ridden over by cabs and vans, injured at fires by falling from ladders, and so on.... The perils which these valuable public servants thus encounter in the protection of the life and property, and the serious injuries which they so often receive in the discharge of their duty, entitle them to a degree of consideration and sympathy on the part of the public, which, however, is rarely extended to them.

Document 25

Hostility to the police in a northern industrial town. *Middlesbrough Weekly News*, 6 January 1865.

[T]he prisoner [Thomas Lougheran] commenced kicking the officer and striking him, [another] four or five men came up and assisted him in committing a most brutal assault. The officer [PC Stainsby] was knocked down, and the men attacked him in the most savage manner, kicking him with their feet, striking him with their sticks, which they carried with them, and biting him. Two severe wounds were inflicted on the top of his head and the officer was rendered well-nigh insensible.

The officer [PC Wilkinson] then took him [Patrick Evans] into custody, when the prisoner called on the crowd to liberate him. Several of his comrades and the prisoner commenced to kick the officer who was presently surrounded by a crowd of 500 to 600 people.

Document 26

Irish opposition to the police. *Middlesbrough Weekly News*, editorial, 6 May 1864.

It has been for a considerable time a practice amongst a certain class to throw every obstruction ... in the way of that exterior machinery of legal administration which has its embodiment in the blue-coated policeman.... Almost weekly cases come under our notice which bear on the surface indications of pecuniary assistance being afforded to criminals by their brother rowdies, and those cases in which their sympathy takes a more active and reprehensible shape are certainly not few and far between. Assaults upon the police, attempts to rescue prisoners, and other and similar interferences placed in the way of the execution of the laws are so frequently taking place that they almost cease to be a matter for comment.... [The offenders] are principally Irishmen of the lowest class.... Such persons regard a policeman as the peregrinating embodiment of tyranny and oppression.

Document 27

Difficulties for the police in rural England. *Dorset County Chronicle*, 16 March 1871. Cited in M. Hann, *Policing Victorian Dorset*, Wincanton, Dorset Publishing, 1989, pp. 54–5.

PC. Hann, who walked with difficulty owing to the injuries he received, and who exhibited his left thumb almost bitten through, said that on Saturday 4th. inst., he in company with PC. Parsons, repaired to the Cross Keys public house, at Cranborne, for the

purpose of apprehending James Zebedee ... Zebedee was at the Cross
Keys very drunk and said that no one should take him to the station.
Thereupon a scuffle ensued; witness and his brother constable
succeeded after some considerable trouble in getting the prisoner out
of the house, upon which John Zebedee came up and struck witness a
terrible blow. They were soon joined by the other prisoners [George
Zebedee, Joseph Bailey, George Bailey and Charles Head], and a
terrible struggle ensued, James Zebedee biting the witness's thumb,
nearly through, and savagely kicking PC. Parsons over the eye,
sending the poor fellow flying several yards across the road. The
severity of the struggle may be imagined when we state that although
the distance between the Cross Keys and the station was only 100
yards, the constables were three-quarters of an hour conveying their
prisoner thither. Witness called for assistance, but, although quite a
hundred people witnessed the struggle, only one, a man named
George Adams, ventured to obey the call.

Document 28

The Metropolitan Police as servants of the public. J. Munro, Late
Commissioner of Police of the Metropolis of London, 'The London
police', *North American Review*, 1890, pp. 617–18.

Weak in numbers as the force is, it would be found in practice
altogether inadequate were it not strengthened, to an extent
unknown, I believe, elsewhere, by the relations which exist between
the police and the public, and by the thorough recognition on the part
of the citizens at large of the police as their friends and protectors.
The police touch all the classes of the public at many points beyond
the performance of the sterner duties as representatives of the law,
and they touch them in a friendly way. Few crossings in crowded
thoroughfares can be got over by the nervous and timid without an
appeal to the courteous help of the policeman; no marriage party in
the West End is complete without the attendance of Scotland Yard to
quietly look after the safety of costly wedding gifts; the laborer in
Whitechapel depends upon the early call of the man on the beat to
rouse him for his work; the police bands often cheer the spirits of
unfashionable audiences in the East End, and the police minstrels are
cordially welcomed at concerts for charitable purposes. Many a
homeless wanderer has to thank the watchful patrol for guiding her
to a 'refuge' for the night, and it is no uncommon sight to see a little
child, lost in the streets, trotting contentedly by the side of a burly

guardian of the peace in a custody as kindly as it is secure.... The police, in short, are not the representatives of an arbitrary and despotic power, directed against the rights or obtrusively interfering with the pleasures of law-abiding citizens: they are simply a disciplined body of men, specially engaged in protecting the 'masses', as well as 'classes' from any infringement of their rights on the part of those who are not law-abiding – a force which is felt to be only a terror to the evil-doer and 'for the praise of them that do well.'

Document 29

Late-nineteenth-century concerns over the growth of the police. E. Carpenter, 'Who will watch the watchmen: a criticism of our police system', *Free Review*, 6, 1896, pp. 144, 147, 149.

The growth of the police in late times, both in numbers and power, is a serious matter requiring grave attention from a people that wishes to remain free and independent. The evils of police systems in foreign countries, culminating perhaps in the bureaucracy of Russia, are common themes: but we do not always ask ourselves how far our own institution is drifting in the same direction.... Taking it as a whole, the system has deepset evils – briberies, tyrannies, iniquities, secrets – which always come in where any class of men is endowed with power over their fellows, but which have to be concealed at all costs....

The large number of recent Acts of a regulative character have led to a considerable increase in the duties of the police, which are sometimes really onerous. Nor in accusing the system need we forget that the individual 'copper' often has some very trying work to perform. But this increase in duties, coupled no doubt with a general feeling of timidity among the authorities with regard to strikes, riots etc., has led to a vast increase in the numbers; and it is easy to see in what direction the whole system is tending.... Is Society really so much afraid of its poor outcasts?

Section 4. Popular responses to the new police

Document 30

Early opposition to the new police in London. Cited in D. Rumbelow, 'Raw lobsters, blue devils', *British Heritage*, 1, 1980, p. 17.

The New Police

PARISHIONERS, – Ask yourselves the following *Questions*:

Why is an Englishman, if he complains of an outrage or an insult, referred for redress to a Commissioner of Police?

Why is a Commissioner of Police delegated to administer justice?

Why are the proceedings of this new POLICE COURT *unpublished* and *unknown*? and by what law of the land is it recognized?

Why is the British Magistrate stripped of his power? and why is Justice transferred from the Justice Bench?

Why is the Sword of Justice placed in the hands of a MILITARY man?

Consider these constitutional questions: consider the additional burthen saddled on you – consider all these points, then UNITE in removing such a powerful force from the hands of Government, and let us institute a Police System in the hands of the PEOPLE under *parochial* appointments –

UNITY IS STRENGTH

THEREFORE,

I, – Let each Parish convene a Meeting.

II, – Let a Committee be chosen, instructed to communicate with other Parishes.

III, – Let Delegates be elected from each Committee to form a
CENTRAL COMMITTEE
To join your brother Londoners in one heart, one hand, for the
Abolition of the New Police

These bills may be had at the Printers, at 4*d*. per dozen; 2*s*. per Hundred, or 17*s*. 6*d*. per Thousand; and the enemies of oppression requested to aid its circulation. ELIOT, Printer, 14 Holywell St. Strand.

Document 31

Troubles in London: Cold Bath Fields, 1833. Report and minutes of evidence of the Select Committee on the Cold Bath Fields Meeting, *Parliamentary Papers*, 1833 (718), xiii, pp. 3–4.

Resolved, THAT it is the Opinion of this Committee, That the conduct of the bodies of Police employed in the actual dispersion of the

Meeting was not attended with greater violence than was occasioned by the resistance they met with, from a portion of the Meeting, in the execution of their orders.

Resolved, THAT it is the Opinion of this Committee, That after the dispersion of the Meeting, some of the Police employed in clearing the surrounding ground were suffered to follow persons to a greater distance than was necessary, and that under these circumstances they were not subjected to that efficient control which, in a moment of excitement and irritation, and after much provocation, could alone prevent individual instances of undue exercise of power.

Resolved, THAT it is the Opinion of this Committee, That none of the Police were in any degree intoxicated and that no dangerous wound or permanent injury has been shown to have been inflicted by them on any individual, while on the other hand one of their own number was killed with a dagger, and two others stabbed while in the discharge of their duty.

Resolved, THAT while it is the Opinion of this Committee, That the conduct of the Police, as a body, on the occasion in question, affords no just ground of complaint, they feel it a duty to advert to the importance of the utmost caution and vigilance on the part of the Superintendents and other Officers of the Police, to check any approach to unnecessary violence among their Men on all occasions, but more especially where large bodies of them are employed in the prevention or suppression of disturbance, and the maintenance of Public Peace.

Document 32

Extracts from the minutes of evidence from the report and minutes of evidence of the Select Committee on the Cold Bath Fields Meeting, *Parliamentary Papers*, 1833 (718), xiii.

Nathaniel Stallwood, resident of Calthorpe-street
Q.255 ... I observed that all those bodies [of police] were formed, and directly afterwards the body which was in Gough-street, that had come out of the stables of Mr. Busbridge, were ordered to draw their truncheons, and immediately that they had done so, the word 'Charge' was given to them, and without any provocation whatever, they immediately attacked those persons that were nearest that spot; the body which was at the end of Calthorpe-street, likewise attacked at the same moment, and they levelled every body without any sort

of distinction whatever, men, women and children, that came in their way.

Q.259 ... they [the police] did nothing but knock them down, break their heads, and punch them in their backs with the end of their truncheon; and if a person turned round to know what it was about, he got a knock first from one and then from another.

John Hudson, Hair-dresser of Little Guildford-street

Q.732 The police came up Calthorpe-street in a sort of military order, and formed themselves in complete lines across the street; and as they came on, condensed, line after line, they took the whole of the street from railing to railing, so that it was impossible, after they had formed round the centre of the street, for any one – entirely impossible for any one to pass them; they must get refuge in the doorways....

Q.736 ... I saw one woman that stood at the door of No. 11 along with me; she made exclamation after the meeting might literally said to be dispersed, and gone towards Bagnigge Wells Road; they were beating some when prostrate on the ground, and she said, 'Consider their wives and families, and do not murder them;' and for that reason three of the policemen came up to the door, No. 11, where she stood along with me, and struck her in the face, and felled her to the ground, and her face bled and they struck me; I was wounded across the head....

Samuel Newton, solicitor's clerk

Q.1086 I saw a man surrounded by eight or ten of the policemen on the opposite side of the way [Calthorpe Street] ... he was bald-headed, and cried out for mercy, and there were about eight or ten of them, and they appeared actually to be striking at him evidently with the desire of bringing him to the ground.

Document 33

Further troubles in London: the Hyde Park Sunday Trading Riots, 1855. *Parliamentary Debates*, 3rd series, 139, 1855, cols 453–4.

Mr. T DUNCOMBE ... The first petition was from inhabitants of Mount Street and Park Street, Grosvenor Square, who expressed their horror and disgust at the brutal and violent conduct of the police in truncheoning the peaceably disposed persons who were attracted to Hyde Park on Sunday.... [Another] petitioner ... stated that his head and face were most dreadfully cut and bruised by the police on

Sunday. The petitioner ... was, with others, brutally driven back from the iron railings by the police, who, having cleared a space of 100 yards in length and ten yards from the railings, nevertheless continued to strike the petitioner and others with their truncheons.... In this way, men, women and children were alike struck by the police, who also beat the petitioner in the most brutal and shameful manner. The petitioner also stated that he saw one woman upon the ground with four or five policemen around her, she having been struck down by their truncheons.

Document 34

Extracts from the Report of H.M. Commissioners on the Alleged Disturbances of the Public Peace in Hyde Park on Sunday July 1st. 1855, *Parliamentary Papers*, 1856 (2016), xxiii, pp. ix, xi.

In entering on the consideration of violence and injuries imputed to the police, we may remark, that there has been no evidence before us of any loss of life or bone broken, of any limb seriously hurt, or permanent injury of any kind inflicted. Seeing that such formidable weapons, as the truncheons of the police undoubtedly are, were used on this occasion, we think there has been some exaggeration in the evidence which describes them as being used with the utmost violence, and so indiscriminately that neither age nor sex was spared.

The conduct of Superintendent Hughes ... has been impugned on several grounds. He has been accused of undue excitement, of using improper language, of having been guilty of many assaults with his horsewhip, and with issuing to the police, without sufficient grounds, orders to use their staves, and with failing to control many excesses on the part of the police under his command....

Weighing all the evidence, however, we think his resort to violence was not warranted. No attack had been made by the people, no combined or serious resistance had been made to the police, the carriages and riders passing were few; and, considering how many inoffensive individuals were mixed up with the disorderly portion of the crowd, the execution of such orders would almost of necessity be dangerous, and attended with unjustifiable violence.

Document 35

Extracts from the minutes of evidence of the Report of H.M. Commissioners on the Alleged Disturbances of the Public Peace in

Hyde Park on Sunday July 1st. 1855, *Parliamentary Papers*, 1856 (2016), xxiii, pp. 28, 220.

William Floyd, second master at the Philological School
Q.825 ... When they made the charge the people from behind me gave way a little, and I had room to step back. Then, however, one of the party seized hold of me. Two of them collared me at each side and tore my coat and waistcoat.

Q.826 Yes, they did [strike me], afterwards, but not till two of them held me; I believe three; I believe one had me by the back of the neck as well. The others crowded around me, and No. 20 came to my right-hand side, and struck me a heavy blow on the right arm while these men were holding me.

Q.828 ... At the same time, two others must have struck me on the left arm, so that they must have gone in a systematic way to work to cripple both arms. I received four blows altogether at the same moment almost, as if they were determined to disable my arms in an instant.

Q.829 ... I noticed 20 once or twice before he called out to me. I saw him look exceedingly savage, as if he were very angry, – in fact, quite out of temper, – long before he made his charge upon me; he was a large, stoutish man, and he particularly attracted my attention.

Robert Ward,
Q.6084 ... The policemen then turned round directly upon the people, and in that affray there was a boy, about I should say, not more than fifteen years of age, who was hit right across the temples, and a life guardsman picked him up and looked the policeman in the face and said, 'You scoundrel, you want a licking, and you ought to be severely punished for this.' I halloed out the policeman's number, but before I could get his number out, he made an attempt to hit me....

J J White, waiter at the William the Fourth, Ship Yard.
Q.6101 I saw an old man knocked down and very much ill-treated by three policemen, who struck him with violence, and the by-standers were crying 'Shame!' and I was too: just as I had done so, something went past me, a small stone or something of the kind, I turned round to see where it came from, I felt a hand on my collar, and I found myself in the hands of policeman 398 A.

Document 36

Criticism of the rural police. *Salopian Telegraph and Border Review*, 6

November 1841. Cited in D. J. Elliot, *Policing Shropshire, 1836–1967*, Studley, Brewin Books, 1984, p. 29.

CORNER FOR THE RURALS

These muckworms have not been quite so busy of late. The Brummagem Button-stick [Superintendent William Baxter of the Shropshire constabulary] is not quite so fast since the check at the Quarter Sessions a short time ago; but he is still as fond of his brandy and pipe, and people generally know where to find him.

As for his underlings they are seen dragging their lazy carcasses about the streets and lanes like so many spies habited in a coarse workhouse livery. Only for their mawkish looks and the absence of fire arms, you would take them for Italian brigands. How these fellows do their duty is well-known, eating and drinking at the expense of hospitable farmers, beer shop keepers and old public houses, instead of looking after the poultry stealers, bad houses, and those ale house keepers who really keep disorderly houses – all these matters are not considered when their bellies have been well stuffed. In short, they are considered a useless burthen on the country, which we hope soon to be rid of.

Document 37

Concerns with police misconduct. *Middlesbrough Weekly News*, (a) 13 August 1859, (b) 23 November 1866, and (c) 19 June 1868.

(a) STREET BRAWLS AND SUNDAY DRINKING. We are glad that the attention of the Town Council has been drawn to this subject. Our streets are the scene of drunkenness and fighting almost every Sabbath and the delinquents evade the punishment of the law and are frequently abetted in their demoralizing practices by the aid of persons who ought to be conservators of peace, instead of exulting in what they are pleased to term 'a good stand up fight.'

(b) I am rather concerned to think what might happen to me were I to walk the streets of Middlesbrough in anything but a black coat, clean collar, shining boots and a conventional 'tile' to complete my outer man.... there is no doubt about the risk, as witness the brutish manner in which Mr. Hudson [a building labourer] was dragged to the police station last week ... Mr. Hobson was dragged through the streets like a felon, in spite of the remonstrances of several tradesmen ... I would always do my best to uphold all lawful authority, that of the Middlesbrough police included, but it will never do to have that authority administered by bullies.

(c) They [the police] were doing an illegal thing in entering the man's house [at midnight].... It reveals a systematic contempt and disregard for the rights and feelings of poor people simply because they are poor.

Document 38

An early-twentieth-century view from Salford. Robert Roberts, *The Classic Slum: Salford Life in the First Quarter of the Century*, London, Penguin, 1971, pp. 93–4, 99–100, 162.

Strike breakers, shielded by the police, attempted to move coal and food. Pickets determined to stop them. In a dozen places fierce fighting broke out that lasted all day. Five hundred policemen from other towns poured in at once.... Beyond the end of our narrow lane we saw huge crowds go milling past in the stifling heat, then, a few minutes later, the rout! Men rushed yelling and cursing into the alley-ways. A score ran towards us, their clogs clattering over the setts, pursued by mounted police. A child, terrified standing by the door, I saw an officer lean forward on his horse and hit a neighbour with his truncheon above the eyes, heard the blow like the thump of wood on a swede turnip. The man ran crouching, hands to his face, into a wall and collapsed. Then my mother grabbed me, screamed after the charging police, fled into the shop and slammed the door. For half a lifetime afterwards the same man stayed among us, but he did little work after. Something about him seemed absent. 'They knocked him silly,' old people said, 'in the dockers' strike.' In one day more than one hundred strikers were treated at hospital for injuries. 'Police charges', explained the newspapers, 'were necessarily vigorous, but officers generally showed a fine restraint under trying circum-stances.'...

Altogether, among the lower working class the actions of the police had left them no better loved than they been before. In 1908 the Chief Constable of Manchester, in his annual report, thought that modern police duty bore 'little resemblance to that of thirty or forty years earlier. Then the policeman dealt largely with the criminal: now he is rendering a public service to all classes'. That he was rendering some sort of service to the poorest of the day there can be not much doubt: during 1908 more than 180,000 of them went to gaol, mostly for

miserable little offences, the highest number in decades.... nobody in
our Northern slum, to my recollection, ever spoke in fond regard,
then or afterwards, of the policeman as 'social worker' and
'handyman of the streets'. Like their children, delinquent or not, the
poor in general looked upon him with fear and dislike. When one
arrived on a 'social' visit they watched his passing with suspicion and
his disappearance with relief....

And in the heart of the group itself, shielded by lounging bodies, a
small card school would sit contentedly gambling for halfpence.
Suddenly one hears a shriek of warning. The gang bursts into a
scatter of flying figures. From nowhere gallop a couple of 'rozzers',
cuffing, hacking, punching, sweeping youngsters into the wall with a
swing of heavy folded capes. The street empties, doors bang.
Breathing heavily the Law retires bearing off perhaps a 'hooligan' or
two to be made an example of. The club is over for another night,
leaving its young members with a fear and hatred of the police that in
some perfectly law-abiding citizens lasted through life and helped
colour the attitude of a whole working-class generation towards civil
authority.

Document 39

A working-class view of the police, 1911. S. Reynolds and B. and T.
Woolley, *Seems So! A Working-Class View of Politics*, London,
Macmillan, 1911, pp. 86–7.

The police are charged not only with the prevention and detection of
crime among them, as among other people, but with the enforcement
of a whole mass of petty enactments, which are little more than social
regulations bearing almost entirely on working-class life. At the
bidding of one class, they attempt to impose a certain social discipline
on another. In every direction, inside his own house as well as out,
the working-man's habits and convenience are interfered with, or his
poverty is penalized by the police. Whether or not he comes into
collision with them is more a matter of good fortune than of law-
abidingness, and he is a lucky man who does not find himself in their
hands at one time or another in his life. Nor can it very well be
otherwise, since the duties of the police have been made to tally with
upper-class, as opposed to working-class, notions of right and wrong;
so that a working man may easily render himself liable to arrest and
all sorts of penalties from hard labour to the loss of a day's work,
without in the least doing what is wrong in his own eyes or in the

opinion of his neighbours. For that reason alone, there is hardly a man who cannot, from the working-class point of view, bring up instances of gross injustice on the part of the police towards himself or his friends or relations – to say nothing of cases that are plainly unjust from any point of view.

Bibliographical essay

Although often criticised for its Whiggish stance, T. A. Critchley, *A History of Police in England and Wales*, London, Constable, 1978 (revised edn; 1st edn 1967), remains a classic survey of policing. However, for an up-to-date analysis of the police from the late eighteenth to the twentieth century, the ousanding work is C. Emsley, *The English Police: A Political and Social History*, Hemel Hempstead, Harvester Wheatsheaf, 1991. A further valuable text, though one that is primarily concerned with modern policing, is R. Reiner, *The Politics of the Police*, 2nd edn, Hemel Hempstead, Harvester Wheatsheaf, 1992. S. H. Palmer, *Police and Protest in England and Ireland, 1780–1850*, Cambridge, Cambridge University Press, 1988, is a detailed study of a crucial period in the evolution of modern policing and provides a useful corrective to the parochialism that often surrounds the study of the English police. C. Steedman, *Policing and the Victorian Community: The Formation of English Provincial Police Forces, 1856–80*, London, Routledge and Kegan Paul, 1984, provides a good survey of the competing models of policing in the mid-nineteenth century.

There are several valuable articles that should be consulted. The overall problem of explaining the emergence of the reformed police in the early nineteenth century is explored perceptively by J. Styles, 'The emergence of the police: explaining police reform in eigtheeth- and nineteenth-century England', *British Journal of Criminology*, 27, 1987. Police reforms are put in a wider context of change in the criminal justice system by D. Philips, 'A new engine of power and authority: the institutionalisation of law enforcement in England, 1780–1830', in V. Gatrell, B. Lenman and G. Parker, eds, *Crime and the Law*, London, Europa, 1980. The myth of inefficiency and corruption among the old police of London is exploded by R. Paley, '"An imperfect, inadequate and wretched system?": policing London before Peel', *Criminal Justice History*, 10, 1989. D. Philips and R. D. Storch, 'Whigs and coppers: the Grey ministry's national police scheme, 1832', *Historical Research*, 67, 1994, throws new light on government thinking in the early 1830s, while R. D. Storch, 'Policing rural southern England before the police: opinions and practice, 1830–1856', in D. Hay and F. Synder, eds, *Policing and Prosecution in Britain, 1750–1850*, Oxford, Oxford University Press, 1989, highlights the degree of experimentation to be found before the passing of the 1856 County and Borough Police Act. The origins of the 1839 Rural Constabulary Act is discussed by A. Brundage, 'Ministers, magistrates and reform: the genesis of the Rural Constabulary Act of 1839', *Parliamentray History*, 5, 1986, and D. Foster, *The Rural Constabulary Act, 1839*, London, Bedford Square Press, 1982.

The creation of efficient police forces is well covered in Steedman, *Policing the Victorian Community*; W. J. Lowe, 'The Lancashire constabulary, 1845–1870: the social and occupational function of a Victorian police force', *Criminal Justice History*, 4, 1983; D. Philips, *Crime and Authority in Victorian England*, London, Croom Helm, 1977; H. Shpayer-Makov, 'The making of a police labour force', *Criminal Justice History*, 24, 1990; R. Swift, 'Urban policing in early Victorian England, 1835–1856: a re-appraisal', *History*, 73, 1988; and D. Taylor, *'A Well-Chosen, Effective Body of Men': The Middlesbrough Police Force, 1841–1914*, Middlesbrough, University of Teesside, Papers in North Eastern History, no. 6, 1995.

R. D. Storch, 'The plague of blue locusts: police reform and popular resistance in northern England, 1840–57', *International Review of Social History*, 20, 1975, and 'The policeman as domestic missionary', *Journal of Social History*, 9, 1976, are seminal articles in the revisionist interpretation. Useful local studies of the role of the new police are to be found in R. Swift, *Police Reform in Early Victorian York, 1835–1856*, University of York, Borthwick Papers, no. 73, 1988, and D. Taylor, 'Crime and policing in early Victorian Middlesbrough, 1835–55', *Journal of Local and Regional Studies*, 11, 1991, but the most entertaining remains B. Davey, *Lawless and*

Immoral: Policing a Country Town, 1835–1857, Leicester, Leicester University Press, 1983. For the later period, S. Petrow, *Policing Morals: The Metropolitan Police and the Home Office, 1870–1914*, Oxford, Oxford University Press, 1994, is an impressive study of the attempts to use the law to change behaviour in London. V. A. C. Gatrell, 'Crime, authority and the policeman-state', in F. M. L. Thompson, ed., *Cambridge Social History*, vol. 3, Cambridge, Cambridge University Press, 1990, is a forcefully argued essay that stresses the increased power of the state in the late nineteenth century and its growing impact on working-class society. R. Samuel, *East End Underworld: Chapters in the Life of Arthur Harding*, London, Routledge and Kegan Paul, 1981, provides a view of the police from the bottom up.

Index

Note: 'n.' after a page reference indicates the number of a note on that page.

Index

County and Borough Police Act (1856), 12, 25, 36–9, 45, 62, 78
county forces
  accountability, 78, 79
  autonomy, 6
  family, 54
  numbers, 45
  recruitment, 47
  turnover, 47
  wages, 70
courts, 15, 96, 126
Crimean War, 37, 87 n. 75
Criminal Justice Act (1826), 15
Critchley, T. A., 2, 77, 80, 124, 173
cruelty to animals, 101, 116
Culley, PC, 9, 98, 99

d'Angely, Eva, 103, 131 n. 46
Davey, B., 174–5
demonstrations, public, 99–100
detection, certainty of, 18
deterrence, *see* prevention of crime
Dimsdale, Thomas, 25
discretion, 90, 94, 138
dismissals, 55–61, 64, 74
diversity, new police, 6, 31, 45, 48
Dixon, Billy, 115
Dixon, George, 64, 136
Dixon of Dock Green, 139 n. 1
Dorset, 30, 55, 57, 70, 92, 161–2
drunkenness
  police, 57–8, 59, 60, 64, 85–6 n. 55
  public, 93–4, 103–4
Dublin, 21, 22, 36
Dudley, Earl of, 19
Duncombe, T. 166–7
Durham, 69, 70, 83 n. 11
Dyer, H. M., 146

East Riding, 29, 51, 53–5, 59–60, 84 n. 37
Edmonds, Edward, 147
education, 66
effectiveness and efficiency of police, 8–9, 75, 78–9, 96, 154–63
emergencies, 123–4
Employers' and Workmen's Act (1875), 91
Emsley, Clive, 4, 7, 173
Engels, Friedrich, 2
Essex, 29, 45, 51, 54, 59
Evans, Patrick, 122–3, 161
experience levels, 65–6
Explosives Act (1861), 80

fairs, 102
family, 49, 53, 54, 55
fear of crime, 5, 6, 13, 14, 40 n. 6
fear of police, 145
firemen, 8
Floyd, William, 168
football, 117
Foster, D., 174
Foster, J., 77
Foucault, Michel, 92
Fox, Charles James, 19

France, 19, 36
Friendly Societies Act (1896), 91
functions of police, 7–8, 89–97, 159

gambling, 94, 103, 104
gang attacks on police, 106–7
Gatenby, Robert, 85–6 n. 55
Gatrell, V. A. C., 16, 96, 105, 174, 175
Gay, William, 113
Gordon Riots (1780), 17, 18, 19
government inspections, 75, 76, 78–9
Greenwood, James, 159
Greig, Major J. J., 94
Griffiths, Thomas, 114

Habitual Criminal Act (1869), 92
habitual criminals, 103
Hann, M., 161–2
Hann, Richard, 55, 92, 114
Hannan, William, 62, 65
Hardwick, J., 145–6
Hart, Judith, 33
Hay, D., 174
Heaton, Superintendent, 93
Henderson, Sir Edmund, 103
holiday entitlements, 53, 74
hours of work, 52–3, 74
Howe Bridge, Battle of (1881), 119
Huddersfield, 35, 93, 128 n. 10
Hudson, John, 166
Hughes, Superintendent, 100, 167
Hull, 51, 54, 58, 69, 110, 111, 120, 128 n. 10, 152
Hyde Park riots (1855), 43 n. 64, 100, 166–8

identity, 75–6
impartiality, police, 102, 118–19, 120
independence, 7
industrial disputes, 118–21
industrialisation, 5, 16
Inebriates Acts (1888, 1898), 104
inspectors, 64, 65
insubordination, 57, 58
Ireland, 21, 22, 36, 110, 123, 132 n. 61
Irish people, 94, 121–3, 161
iron and steel industry, 50, 71, 72
isolation, 51, 52, 54–5

Jay, Reverend Osborne, 106
Jennings' Buildings, 94, 108
Jervis, Richard, 55, 76, 85 n. 52, 119
Jewitt, Alfred, 55
journals, in-house, 75, 76
justices of the peace, 23, 31
juveniles, 95, 97

Kent, 29, 30, 31
knockers-up, 8, 68
Knowlson, Frederick, 66

Lancashire, 29
  appearance of policemen, 54
  assaults on policemen, 106, 119
  guidance, 155–6
  isolation of policemen, 55

Index

length of service, 62
levels of crime, 96
number of policemen, 45
police:population ratios, 33
recruitment, 48, 49, 50
resignations and dismissals, 55–7
turnover rates, 46, 83 n. 11
wages, 70
Layard, Major, 59
Lee, Captain W. L., 140–1
Leeds, 32–3, 106, 110–11, 128 n. 10
Improvement Act (1842), 128 n. 10
Lefevre, Charles Shaw, 27
Lenman, B., 174
levels of crime, 14–15, 96–7
liberty and order, balance between, 13, 17, 19,
23, 39, 75, 145
Licensing Act (1872), 103, 118
Lighting and Watching Act (1833), 25
Liverpool
accountability, 80, 81
brewing interest, 87 n. 76
constabulary duties, 93, 94, 97
Municipal Corporations Act (1835), 32
number of policemen, 45
popular responses, 120
wages, 70
Liverpool, Lord, 20, 21
living standards, 70, 97, 138
Local Government Act (1888), 78, 87 n. 75
London
County and Borough Police Act (1856), 38
dangers, 160
levels of crime, 96
Metropolitan Police Act (1829), 14–22
number of policemen, 45
popular response, 8, 97–108, 163–4
watch-system, 146
see also Metropolitan Police Force
long-service class, 64, 65, 71
long-term policemen, 44, 61–77, 137
Lowe, W. J., 174
Luton, 54, 84 n. 37

Macleod, Superintendent, 108–9
Macready, General, 120
magistrates
accountability to, 6, 79
attitudes towards, 18
constabulary duties, 93
limitations, 19
recruitment of police, 31
Rural Constabulary Act (1839), 29
Manchester
assaults on policemen, 106
constabulary duties, 128 n. 10
number of policemen, 45
policing crisis, 36
popular responses, 110, 111
Reform Riots, 35
reforms, reactions to, 23
size of police force, 32
wages, 69, 70
Mann, George, 66

marital status of recruits, 48–9
Marx, Karl, 2
masculinity, redefinition of, 97
Mawer, Mathew, 66
Mayhew, Henry, 105, 106
Mayne, Sir Richard, 36, 57, 90, 95, 99, 100
mayor, 77
McHardy, Captain J. B. B., 158
meal breaks, 74
Melbourne, Viscount, 23, 31, 32
merit class, 71
Metropolis Police Improvement Bill (1829), 14,
21, 149–50
Metropolitan Police Act (1829), 12, 16, 21, 22,
101
Metropolitan Police Force
accountability, 77–8
functions, 7
General Instructions, 90, 101
Metropolitan Police Act (1829), 14–22
perks, 86 n. 63
popular response, 99, 103, 104, 107–8, 120
public servant role, 162–3
recruits, 49
resignations and dismissals, 57, 61
short-term emergencies, 35
size, 45
training, 51
turnover, 46
wages, 69
Metropolitan Radical Association, 100
Metropolitan Streets Act (1867), 101, 131 n. 49
middle class, 39
accountability of police, 6, 77
constabulary duties, 95
and functions of police, 8
popular response to police, 9, 75, 98, 124,
126, 138
public servant image, 76
Middlesbrough
constabulary duties, 93–4, 128 n. 11
earnings, 71–4
Improvement Act (1841), 61–2, 118, 128 n. 10
long-term policemen, 64–6, 67
misconduct, 169–70
popular responses, 112–13, 122, 123
recruitment, 50
resignations and dismissals, 57, 58 74, 85 n. 40
training, 51
turnover rates, 46, 63
unity, 75
Middlesex Justices Act (1792), 19
migrant workers, 94–5
military, *see* army
Miller, Wilbur, 98
minimal force, 95, 129 n. 19, 138
misconduct, police, 169–70
modernisation, 2, 16–17
morals, public, 91, 93, 101, 107
Morrison, Arthur, 106
moving-on system, 99, 108, 118
Municipal Corporations Act (1835), 12, 31–5,
42 n. 58, 43 n. 59, 45, 77
Munro, J., 162–3

178

Index

Napier, Sir Charles, 28, 109
Napoleonic Wars, 17, 37
National Anti-Gambling League, 104
National Political Union, 99
Navigation Street gang, 113
neglect of duty, 57, 58, 60, 64
neo-Reithian synthesis, 4, 41 n. 24, 143
Newton, Samuel, 166
Night Poaching Act (1862), 91
Norfolk, 25, 26, 29, 51, 52–3, 123–4
North Riding, 61, 71, 83 n. 11
Norwich, 49, 52, 80
Nott-Bower, W., Head Constable of Liverpool, 81, 94
Nottingham, 23, 35, 83 n. 11
number of forces, 45
number of policemen, 20, 32–3, 34–5, 45, 96

occupational background, 47–8, 49
Oldham, 35, 43 n. 59, 58–9, 79, 86, 115, 128 n. 8
organised labour, 8
orthodox historians, 2, 5, 106, 141, 143
    accountability and consent, 77, 82
    functions of police, 7, 8
    increasing crime levels, 14, 22
    limitations of views, 3, 4, 6
    popular response to police, 9, 124
    prevention of crime, 90
    watchmen, incompetence, 15
Orwell, George, 1
outcast groups, 92, 102

Paley, Ruth, 15, 174
Palmer, S. H., 21, 173
Palmerston, Viscount, 37
Parish Constable Acts (1842, 1850), 30
parish constables, 30
Parker, G., 174
Parsons, PC, 161–2
Peace Preservation Police, 35–6
Peacock, William, 66
Peel, Sir Robert, 5, 16, 36
    crime statistics, 40 n. 6
    Criminal Justice Act (1826), 15
    Metropolitan Police Act (1829), 14, 21, 149–50
    national police force, 23
    public order problem, 20, 21
    punishment, nature of, 18
    Select Committee on the Police of the Metropolis, 19, 21
Peel House, 51
Penal Servitude Act (1853), 37
pensions, 68, 69, 74
perks, 68
Petrow, S., 104, 175
petty crime, 27, 97, 107, 115
Philips, D., 173–4
Pitt, William, 'the Younger', 18, 21
Police Act (1826), 43 n. 59
Police (Expenses) Act (1874), 78
Police Manual, 51, 66–7, 57–8
police:population ratios, 33, 34–5, 45
Police Review and Parade Gossip, 75

Police Service Advertiser, 75
Poor Law, 24, 26, 27, 29, 35 68, 113
Popay, Sergeant, 99
popular response, 7, 9–10, 74–5, 82, 124–7, 138, 160–1, 163–72
    London, 97–108
    provinces, 108–24
poverty,49
power, police, 91, 101, 104, 138
Preston, 35, 70, 119, 121
prevention of crime, 30, 39, 9, 148–9, 154, 155
    changing emphasis, 17, 96,101
    detection, certainty of, 18
Prevention of Crime Act (1871), 92
private lives, policemen, 53
private subscription forces, 25–6
professionalism, 76
promotion, 64–5, 68, 72
property rights, 17
proportionate punishment, 17
prosecutions, 14–15, 26, 96
prostitution, 102–3
public houses, 117–18
public opinion, *see* popular responses
public relations, 95
public servant role, 7–8, 162–3
punishment, changing nature of, 17–18

radicalism, 21, 22, 35, 38, 99, 121–2
Radzinowicz, Sir Leon, 2
Raison, Enoch, 114–15
Ratcliffe Highway murders, 19
Raywell Road Riots (1870), 111
recruitment, 47–50, 158
Reed, John, 66
Reform Riots (1829–32), 24, 33–5, 98
Regan, Brigit, 112
rehabilitation, 17
Reiner, Robert, 4, 7, 41 n. 24, 143, 173
Reith, Charles, 2, 12, 98, 124, 141
religion, 53–4
resignations, 55–61, 74
rest days, 53
revisionist historians, 2–4, 5–6, 39, 141–2, 143
    accountability and consent, 77, 82
    functions of police, 8
    limitations of views, 6
    popular response to police, 9
Reynolds, S., 124–5, 134 n. 90, 171–2
Richmond, A. B., 146–7
Richmond, Duke of, 27
Roberts, M. J. D., 101
Roberts, Robert, 111, 121, 170–1
Rochdale, 43 n. 59, 118
Rowan, Colonel, 27, 57, 90, 95, 99
Rural Constabulary Act (1839), 12, 26, 27–30, 31, 42–3 n. 58, 43 n. 59, 78, 153
rural policing, 24–31, 151–2, 158, 161, 168–9
Russell, Lord John, 27, 28, 32
Russia, 163

Saggerson, Edward, 66, 128 n. 17, 122
Salford, 106, 111, 170–1
Sample, Andrew, 66

Index

Samuel, R., 175
security, police work, 74
Select Committee on the Cold Bath Fields Meeting, 99, 164–6
Select Committee on the Petition of Frederick Young and Others, 99
Select Committee on Police, 152–4
Select Committee on the Police of the Metropolis, 19–20, 21, 144–5, 146–8
Select Committee on Police Superannuation Funds, 47, 49, 57
self-discipline, 51, 52, 53, 61
self-image, 75, 76
sergeants, 64, 86 n. 68
sexual misconduct, 58–9
Sheffield, 32, 50, 79
Shelburne, Lord, 18
Shpayer-Makov, H., 174
Shropshire, 27–8, 53, 59, 84 n. 37, 114, 169
Sidmouth, Viscount, 20
Smethurst, Thomas, 111
Smiles, Samuel, 160
social control, 3, 5–6, 7, 26, 126
special constables, 36
Special Constables Act (1836), 30
Staffordshire, 29, 42 n. 49, 46, 47–8, 49, 56, 62, 115
Stainsby, PC, 122, 161
Stallwood, Nathaniel, 165–6
statistics, crime, 14–15, 37, 96, 106
Steedman, C., 37–8, 173, 174
stereotypes, criminal, 95, 121, 123
Stockport, 33, 36, 79, 93
Storch, Robert D., 8, 25, 77, 90, 141–3, 174
Street Betting Act (1906), 131 n. 49
street traders, 105, 118
Styles, John, 13, 173
subscription forces, 25–6
Suffolk, 26, 29, 58
Summary Jurisdiction Act (1879), 91
Summary Jurisdiction (Married Women) Act (1885), 91
superintendents, 64
superintending constables, 30
Swift, R., 174
Swing Riots (1830/31), 23, 24, 25–6, 29
Synder, F., 174

Taylor, D., 174
Tenbury, Vicar of, 26
Thompson, E. P. 17
Thompson, Flora, 55, 125
Thompson, F. M. L., 3, 175
Thorpe, Robert, 66
ticket-of-leave system, 37
Titchman, Robert, 49
Town Police Clauses Act (1847), 36
traditions, 115–17
training, 51, 66
transfers, 55, 85 n. 42
turf fraud case (1877), 104
turnover rates, 45–7, 50–1, 65

unemployment, 49, 108

uniform, 53, 54, 68
upper class, 39, 171
 accountability to new police, 6
 diminishing tolerance of poor, 17
 national policing, 25
 response to police, 124, 126, 138
urbanisation, 5, 16
urban policing, 31–6, 45, 158–9, 160–1
 see also London; Metropolitan Police Force

Vagrancy Act (1822), 101
violence
 against police, 9, 99–100, 105–15, 117–19, 122–3, 138, 160, 162
 by police, 58, 95, 100, 119, 129 n. 19, 166, 168, 170
 interpersonal, 97, 138

wages, 49–50, 57, 64, 69, 69–74, 158, 159
Ward, Robert, 168
Warden, J. H., 42 n. 34
Warner, Major Ashton, 49
Warner, Jack, 139 n. 1
Warren, Sir Charles, 103, 131 n. 44
watch committees
 accountability to, 6, 77–8, 79–80, 81
 constabulary duties, 92–3, 94
 Municipal Corporations Act (1835), 32
 wage levels, 69
watchmen, 149, 150, 152
 inadequacies, 5, 14, 15–16, 22, 146–7
 Lighting and Watching Act (1833), 25
weights and measures, inspectors of, 8
Wellington, Duke of, 20, 150
West Riding, 29, 45, 83 n. 11, 93, 106, 110
Whig historians, *see* orthodox historians
Whigs
 County and Borough Police Act (1856), 8–9
 Poor Law, 24
 reform discussions, 23, 35, 150–1
 rural policing, 27
 urban policing, 31
White, J. J., 168
Whittlesey, 117
Wigan, 33, 36, 119
Wilkinson, PC, 161
Wilson, Isaac, 50
Wine and Beerhouses Act (1869), 103, 117–18
Woolley, B., 124–5, 134 n. 90, 171–2
Woolley, T., 124–5, 134 n. 90, 171–2
Woodford, J., 156
working class, 39, 127
 constabulary duties, 90
 incorporation into political life, 138
 and isolation of policemen, 54–5
 living standards, 97
 popular response to police, 9, 75, 98, 99, 105, 107, 113, 124, 126, 170–2
 revisionism, 3
working conditions, 52–3, 74, 86–7 n. 69
Wymondham, 25, 27, 152

yeomanry, 20, 22
York, 38, 52, 69, 78–9, 93, 97, 114, 121

180